W9-BJN-517

FIVE CRIES OF YOUTH

FIVE

CRIES

OF

YOUTH

Merton P. Strommen

Published in San Francisco by
Harper & Row, Publishers

New York, Hagerstown, San Francisco, London

To my sons Peter, Tim, Jim, John, and David
who have given me much companionship and joy

FIVE CRIES OF YOUTH. Copyright © 1974, 1979 by Merton P. Strommen. All rights reserved. Printed in the United States of America. No part of this book may be used or reproduced in any manner whatsoever without written permission except in the case of brief quotations embodied in critical articles and reviews. For information address Harper & Row, Publishers, Inc., 10 East 53rd Street, New York, N.Y. 10022. Published simultaneously in Canada by Fitzhenry & Whiteside Limited, Toronto.

First Harper & Row paperback edition published in 1979.

83 84 85 86   10 9 8 7 6

Library of Congress Cataloging in Publication Data

Strommen, Merton P
  Five cries of youth.
  Bibliography: p. 151.
    1. Youth—Conduct of life—Case studies.
2. Youth—Religious life—Case studies. I. Title.
BJ1661.S9   170′.202′23   73-19690
ISBN 0-06-067748-1

Contents

Figures

Tables

Acknowledgments

I wish to thank Lilly Endowment for assistance in funding the Youth Ministry Training Study, of which this book is a part. One objective of that study was to identify the pressing needs of denominational youth through a series of national youth surveys. Mr. Charles Williams of Lilly Endowment was most supportive and encouraging throughout the project.

I wish to thank also the persons listed below who carried primary responsibility for the survey of their youth.

Roman Catholic—Rev. William Friend
Southern Baptist—Dr. James Daniel
               Dr. James Lowry
American Baptist—Dr. Richard Gladden
               Rev. John Carroll
United Methodist—Rev. Charles Courtoy
Evangelical Covenant—Rev. Aaron Markuson
Orthodox Church in America—Ms. Constance Tarasar
Mennonite—Dr. Paul Lederach
Young Life—Mr. Ken Wright
Lutheran—Dr. Milo Brekke
Episcopal—Ms. Ruth Cheney

A special acknowledgment goes to the National Institute of Mental Health, sponsor of the studies to which frequent reference is made in this book—Clergy-Youth Counseling Project (#16460) and Youth Reaching Youth (#17015–01). I served as principal investigator for both studies. Dr. Howard Davis has by his interest in these projects demonstrated the concern of leaders in government for projects which they sponsor.

Acknowledgment also goes to Lutheran Brotherhood, a fraternal benefit society, for their generous contribution of computer time, without which this ecumenical venture would not have been possible.

Special thanks to: my wife, Irene, for helping me with the first draft manuscripts; Dorothy Williams for sharing her writing skill in the illustrative characterizations; Solveig Heintz for typing seemingly endless tables and revisions; and Shelby Andress for her careful copyediting. Thanks also to Dr. Ram Gupta and his assistant, Dr. Peter Braun of Edmonton, Canada, for their help in constructing the research instrument. My gratitude also goes to Ernest Thompson for his help in data analysis and to Dr. Milo Brekke for his research expertise and counsel. These members of the Youth Research Center, as well as others listed above, were invaluable in helping to produce this book.

I am deeply grateful to my mentor, doctoral advisor, and close friend, Dr. C. Gilbert Wrenn. His astute critique of in-process revisions and warm support of the writing project are illustrative of the way this man has shared his life with others.

My thanks to Nancy Nelson, a personal friend, for granting me permission to use three of her poems.

And finally, special appreciation to the Study Committee on Youth Leaders and Training: Drs. Sara Little, Francis Gamelin, and Robert Menges. I am indebted to these colleagues for sage counsel and provocative leadership in the field of education. Books they are preparing will treat important areas in youth work, not touched in *Five Cries of Youth*.

—MERTON P. STROMMEN
President, Youth Research Center

Preface to the Paperback Edition

Assuming that youth in one time period differ at least somewhat from those in another time, have the major characteristics of youth changed since this book first appeared in 1974, or are its descriptions still valid?

Our survey data—collected in 1970, 1971, 1974, and 1977—show what has remained constant, where change has occurred, and the extent of the change. The trend disclosed by the data indicates that the five cries described in this book continue to be the preoccupation of a significant portion of church youth. The principal changes uncovered are in the number of youth who identify with the cries of social protest and of joy. Fewer youth in 1977 were disturbed over matters of injustice and human suffering than in 1970; fewer were troubled to the point of protest. On the other hand, more youth in 1977 were finding satisfaction in a personal faith; their interest and involvement in congregational life was on the increase. This greater commitment to a personal faith is not paralleled by a withdrawal from a life of service, however. The value youth give to a service-oriented life remained the same over the seven-year period.

The Youth Research Survey questionnaire, by which our data were gathered, continues to be used in the congregations and schools of many denominations. The long form (described on pages 4-6) has in many cases been replaced by a shortened version, measuring only fifteen of the twenty-five characteristics discussed in this book. (Those omitted in the mini-survey were deemed less significant in content or found to be less reliable measures for personal counseling than the others.) Comparisons which follow are based on the fifteen scales of the mini-survey.

The youth whose survey responses we report here took part because their Catholic, Lutheran, or Baptist school or congregation—throughout the United States—decided to use the youth survey. Though the participants do not yield a random sample of their denomination, their responses provide substantial evidence of how youth in these denominations did or did not change between 1970 and 1977.

Profile of Participants

| | Number of Youth | | | |
Year	Catholic	Lutheran	Baptist	Total
1970-71	5562	1900	2064	9526
1974	2982	1007	770	4759
1977	3805	1396	1682	6883

Inasmuch as these denominations differ in many ways, it is reasonable to expect these three groups to yield differing scores. Hence, when their findings are combined into a single score—as they are in this updating—scores that remain the same over time are especially noteworthy.

Cry of Self-Hatred

Six of the eight dimensions forming this cry (see Chapter 2) are updated here. Striking evidence shows that five of these concerns—personal faults, lack of self-confidence, classroom relationships, God relationships, and family unity—exhibit no change over a period of seven years within any of the denominational groups. Their standardized scores do not vary as much as one single point from 1970 to 1977.

Only the sixth measure, self-regard, shows a significant change, increasing 2.1 standard points in the seven-year period. This increase, though significant, is outweighed by the lack of change among the other five measures. This change alone is not great enough to assume that descriptions presented in Chapter 2 need to be altered. In general, the cry of self-hatred was given with the same intensity and by the same number of youth in 1977 as in 1970.

Cry of Psychological Orphans

Two of the four dimensions of this cry are included in the update: parental understanding and lack of family unity. Scores for these concerns also remained the same over the seven-year period, not varying more than half a point at any time. Thus there is strong reason to believe that what is reported in Chapter 3 continues to be a fitting description of the poignant cry that characterizes one out of five church youth.

Cry of Social Protest

Updated information is available on three of the five facets of youth's concern over current social issues: human relations, orientation for change, and national issues.

The one measure showing a significant drop (i.e., two or more standard points) relates to concern over such matters as injustice, pollution of land and water, and world hunger. The drop is from a score of 49.7 in 1970, to 45.2 in 1974 and 45.6 in 1977. The drop of 4.1 standard points is not only of statistical but practical significance.

This notable drop in concern over national issues indicates that the cry of social protest (Chapter 4) was expressed by fewer church youth in 1977. Though basically the same proportion of youth felt kindly toward people commonly condemned (see human relations) and toward social and political change (see orientation to change), there was a decided lessening of concern over social issues.

Cry of the Prejudiced

Half of this cry's six dimensions are included in the updating:

human relations, biblical concepts, and national issues. The key characteristics of this cry, assessed by the human relations and biblical concepts scales, show a change of less than two standard points. Though it is true that the third measure, national issues, shows a drop in concern, that issue must be viewed as contributing little to the cry (see page 82). One can conclude that the cry of the prejudiced (Chapter 5) continues to be an accurate description of a small group of youth.

Cry of the Joyous

The area of greatest change since 1970 is the cry of joy (described in Chapter 6); a notable shift took place over the seven-year period. In 1977, more youth indicated greater religious participation, a heightened awareness of a personal God, and an increased self-regard. More youth intensified their commitment to Christ and became more involved in the life of their congregation. The evidence is that the cry has not changed, though the number who identify with it is greater.

Note that though youth's sense of moral responsibility rose in 1974, the score for 1977 showed no significant increase over 1970. Note also the fact that, while youth's concern over national issues decreased, their desire for a meaningful life of service did not.

Scores on Five Characteristics of Joy, by Update Sample
1970-1977

Characteristic	1970-71	1974	1977
Religious Participation	50.8	53.6	54.3*
Awareness of Personal God	49.3	53.6	53.7*
Self-Regard	50.6	52.0	52.7*
Sense of Moral Responsibility	50.6	53.3	51.7
Desire for Meaningful Life	50.4	51.6	50.0
Total number of youth sampled	N=9526	N=4759	N=6883

*Significant increases over 1970

Preface to the First Edition

The Questions

Many parents find that their children's adolescence breeds sleepless nights full with questions. Why has Paul shut us out of his life? Am I too strict? What can I do about the way John is rebelling? Will Jenny ever show interest in a religious faith?

While parents are asking one set of questions, adult leaders in congregations are asking related ones. Are we dealing with a "new breed" in this generation? Does a personal faith make a difference in the lives of American youth? Are the "loyalists" in church youth groups primarily "losers"? Has the pressure cooker of today's living made anxiety a serious issue? Should I take youth's critiques of the church seriously? What can I do about prejudice? What is a healthy religious faith?

This book proposes to apply hard-nosed research to these questions and to indicate directions in which youth ministry ought to go. It is offered in full awareness of the fact that it differs from the conclusions of some highly visible writers on certain youth problems; its claim to authority rests in the previously unavailable research data which have guided my interpretation. These data collected from national samples of church youth have been organized according to highly complex and sophisticated research procedures.

The Focus

In this book you hear the voice of American church youth, who comprise two-thirds of the total population of American young people. These youth, ages fourteen to eighteen, who identify with a United States church body and represent millions of high-school youth, include the dormant and disinterested as well as the vital and active members. In these pages you hear self-reports of their values, beliefs, and opinions and their concerns about themselves, their friends, their world, and their God. If you listen, you can hear cries, rising out of the data with compelling insistence; sobs, angry shouts, hurrahs, protests, and jeers.

The cries which underlie the self-reports of 7,050 representative youth challenge the adequacy of a youth ministry that is all evangelism, all social involvement, all socializing activities, or all doctrinal instruction. They posit five basic needs or value orientations, requiring five distinct accents in a youth ministry.

The Two Emphases

This book does more than report and summarize the research; it also attempts to catch the significance of youth's cries and point toward ways of responding to them. Beyond objective research facts, it offers an interpretation reflecting my biases and theological stance.

I am doubtful about the claims of those who predict a doleful future for the church. This study and others like it (*A Study of Generations*, 1973, and the *National Council of Churches Study*, 1972) attest to a vigorous core of committed Christians who reflect in their values, beliefs, and behavior the power of a personal faith. Most church members, youth as well as adults, are hopeful about the future and convinced of the importance of their congregation's mission. This is reflected in the hopeful stance of this book. I believe that one finds in Jesus Christ the alpha and omega of life.

Throughout this book you will find two emphases which are

usually strangers. One is upon rigorous, objective research; the second is upon establishing a rationale for the findings and identifying what is important for the parent and youth leader. It is my hope that this book will encourage a more thoughtful and sustained approach to a home and congregational youth ministry.

Missing in this report are the technical explanations of research procedures and the documentary evidence of tabular data that a research scholar expects. These are available from the author in a series of 29 tables and a full description of research procedures. This book is not a scientific report but rather the development of a rationale that is informed by research findings gathered over a period of years.

So runs my dream.
And what am I?
An infant, crying in the night
An infant, crying for the light,
And with no language but a cry?
from "In Memoriam"

1   To Hear and Understand the Cries

Sometimes I cry
I am sorry,
   but I do.
         Nancy Nelson, age seventeen

Young people, like the rest of us, cry out their needs in many puzzling ways. Some are extremely critical of everyone and everything around them; some plunge into a flurry of service activities or secede from the world by spending every possible moment before the TV. Some turn their backs on friends and family, seeming to shut them out. Others surround themselves with a screen of cheerful insults, jokes, and high-pitched laughter. Still others are caught in a new religious ardor that seems unnatural to their parents.

Because of the indirect ways in which youth speak to us, their cries are often mistaken for something else. But all of them can be expressive of deep human needs which are hard to articulate.

Persons who sincerely care about young people must not ignore these disguised pleas for direction, help, and understanding, difficult as they are to interpret.

This book is written as an aid to hearing and interpreting the cries. The survey data on which it is based were collected from 7,050 high-school students during the spring and summer of 1970. These were randomly selected from more than a dozen church denominations, from Young Life groups, and from groups with no discernible religious affiliation.

In 1970, student unrest and campus violence were at their peak, not only in colleges throughout the country, but in high schools and even in some junior high schools. The survey data produced a snapshot of church youth's attitudes at a time when dissatisfaction with adult institutions was prevalent among young people. It was an unprecedented time in America's history, frightening to many adults, when the cries of youth were audible and insistent as never before.

Is This Book Necessary?

Until recently there was little information on the attitudes, concerns, interests, beliefs, and values of young people who are members of religious institutions. I became aware of this while serving as editor of the comprehensive handbook *Research on Religious Development* (1971). When Havighurst and Keating (coauthors of a chapter in the handbook) combed the material published over four decades, they found little solid research on youth where religion is included as a variable. Of the many chapters set aside for specialized topics and specific age groups, none was as lacking in published research as the chapter on church youth of high-school age. This book is intended to supply facts where before we had only myths, assumptions, and individual experiences. It supplies a map of territory which those who care about youth must travel. There is no neatly marked route, but landmarks—high ground, swamp, forest, and thicket. With facts in hand, we can make more informed choices for the journey.

I have one concern over classifying youth as I do in this book. The danger is that some readers will use the categories to label individuals and then treat them according to that category.

Our division into five cries does not imply that a given individual can belong to only one group; he may be troubled by both family pressures and low self-esteem. Church youth do not come tidily sectioned off with one problem apiece—which, of course, makes them additionally individual.

One way of handling this problem is to dismiss all attempts to understand the human person in a broad, general way; it is enough to focus on an individual, come to know his uniqueness, and respond accordingly.

Every young person is unique; he has special needs, interests, and potentialities.

But how does one minister to groups of 100 (or even 50) young people in a congregation or church-sponsored school? Must there be 100 different approaches? What about common needs in groups of young people? Is it possible to minister to these categories while recognizing and making allowances for the uniqueness of each person?

Counterculture youth differ from high-school athletes in their values and attitudes toward authority. Young people from tragic home situations contrast with those from happy homes. Youth must be approached in differing ways because they vary in their views of themselves and life. This does not require stereotyping or labeling, but only sensitivity to the likely meanings of behavioral patterns.

I am not advocating a problem approach to youth. The issue is not: What is John's problem? but What sort of person is John? How can we help him find his potential and the fullest enjoyment of life? Our task is to collaborate with a young person in discovering ways to solve his own problems.

To understand his cries is to know where to begin. Solutions emerge in an atmosphere of mutuality (the warmth and interaction of accepting persons) and in the challenge of collaborative activities which lead to a sense of mission in life.

This brings me to what I hope you gain through reading this book.

First, I hope you will hear with greater clarity the individual cries implicit in the behavior of young people. The ability to hear does not come quickly and naturally. It is a sensitivity one must learn, as a musician learns to distinguish instruments in a symphony orchestra, or as an auto mechanic becomes sensitive to the healthy and unhealthy sounds produced by running engines.

Second, I hope you will increase your understanding of what

you hear by developing a framework of meaning. If you awaken at night and hear the front door open and close, it is your background of knowledge that causes you to leap to your feet or simply go back to sleep. Is everyone at home and in bed? Is one member still out? The understanding with which you hear the cries of youth gives meaning to what you hear and can help you determine which cries deserve your first attention.

How Do You Make Sense of the Data?

How was it possible to listen to thousands of descriptions of concerns, values, attitudes, beliefs, and behavior and make sense out of that flood of communication? The Youth Research Center Survey has 420 items, developed over a twelve-year period of use and selected for their success in outlining the significant and troublesome areas of a young person's life. In response, the young people gave us three million bits of information—an enormous jigsaw puzzle whose cover picture was missing.

Running through the responses we found over twenty-five common threads or characteristics. One characteristic cluster of items centered on family unity, another on personal faults, and a third on youth's concern over national issues and so on. Listed below are these twenty-five clusters or characteristics by which youth describe themselves and sketch their profiles.[1]

CONCERNS

1. FAMILY UNITY: Concern over an apparent lack of love and oneness in the family.
2. PARENTAL UNDERSTANDING: Feelings about a lack of understanding and acceptance between youth and parents.
3. FAMILY PRESSURES: Extent to which external factors (illness, absence of father, financial problems, etc.) are present to intensify negative reactions in the home.
4. LIFE PARTNER: Degree to which youth wonder or think about finding the "right one" to marry.
5. LACK OF SELF-CONFIDENCE: Degree to which one is anxious about making mistakes and being ridiculed by others.
6. ACADEMIC PROBLEMS: Concern over school studies and one's ability. A fear of failing to do as well as one should.
7. PERSONAL FAULTS: Disappointment over not having lived up to one's ideals of personal living. Feelings of guilt.

8. CLASSROOM RELATIONSHIPS: A feeling of not being accepted by others while at school, that one is an outsider, lonely and unnecessary to a group.
9. NATIONAL ISSUES: Fear over what is happening nationwide coupled with a deep sensitivity to current injustices.
10. GOD RELATIONSHIP: A feeling of being out of touch with God and being troubled by it.

BELIEFS - VALUES

11. INTEREST IN HELP: Degree to which one might expect youth to participate in opportunities provided by the church.
12. MATURITY OF VALUES: Perceived ability to delay immediate drives and resist outer pressures in favor of moving toward goals of one's own choosing.
13. ORIENTATION FOR CHANGE: Degree to which youth's opinions on national issues tend to be more or less liberal in comparison to traditional attitudes.
14. MORAL RESPONSIBILITY: Degree of importance youth give to being their brother's keeper and living under a sense of God's authority.
15. MEANINGFUL LIFE: Importance accorded a life of service, responsible living toward others, meaningful work, wisdom, honesty, a relationship with God, and giving and receiving love.
16. RELIGIOUS PARTICIPATION: Degree of involvement in the life, faith, and activities of the institutional church.
17. SOCIAL ACTION: Extent to which youth are helping through small deeds of kindness and participating in activities labeled social action.
18. SELF-REGARD: Degree to which youth accept themselves as persons of worth and possibility.
19. HUMAN RELATIONS: Attitudes of openness and kindness toward people of different nationalities, race, or religion.
20. GOD AWARENESS: Extent to which youth are aware of God in their lives and believe that he is an ever present reality.
21. BIBLICAL CONCEPTS: Extent to which youth reject statements of a generalized religion and, in doing so, reflect their perception of a particularized, biblical faith.

PERCEPTION

22. YOUTH GROUP VITALITY: Degree to which the youth are impressed by the climate of acceptance and sense of mission that characterizes their church youth group.
23. ADULT CARING: Extent to which the youth are impressed by the attitudes of caring and concern that characterize the adult congregation.
24. FAMILY SOCIAL CONCERNS: Youth's perception of the extent to which their parents and family are responsive to human need and involved in helping activities.
25. FRANKNESS: Openness in admitting what is uncomplimentary.

These twenty-five recognizable characteristics organize themselves into five distinct and quite interpretable groups or constellations. Through a computer process known as second order factor analysis the magnetic attraction of one characteristic for its closest relatives produces these clusters.[2] Each combination of characteristics defines an area of great concern in the lives of young people:

Self-Esteem
Family Unity and Well-Being
Welfare of People
Achieving Favor
Personal Faith

How Authoritative Are the Data?

The detailed answer to this question can be found in another publication, *Manual for Youth Research Survey: Section 4* (Strommen and Gupta 1971).

The data closely approximate what is broadly or generally true in fact. Of course, optical scanners cannot always read the marks of youthful respondents; persons who describe their feelings are not always accurate in what they say about themselves; the sample is not a precise random one drawn in proportion to the size of all denominational groups, etc. But the empirical checks reported in the *Manual* show the data to be highly reliable and valid.

Underlying the discussion in this book are three assumptions—

1. that young people can be insightful and their reports valid; that they can report the conscious derivatives of unconscious motivations; that defense mechanisms, self-deception, rationalization do not dominate most young people enough to invalidate their total self-report;
2. that adolescent psychodynamics are evidenced by verbally expressed problems which tend to cluster symptomatically around an underlying concern (this means that from problem-items can be inferred psychologically significant concerns);
3. that a knowledge of youth's concerns is important to an effective youth ministry (unless information is related to real interests and has immediate meaning it will be forgotten or perceived in distorted form).

Three cautions. First, this book is based on one kind of research data, namely, self-report. This means that our knowledge is limited to what church youth *said* they believe, value, opine, and do.

Second, the data are cross-sectional in time and limited to correlational information; therefore, the data cannot identify trends or tell what *caused* what.

Third, groups formed by the cries do overlap. Though most youth express predominantly one cry, some youth make several cries in somewhat equal proportions.

Who Are the Young People in the Study?

In this book, you listen to a nationwide group of high-school age youth, randomly selected from among American Baptist, Roman Catholic (parochial school), United Methodist, Southern Baptist, and Young Life participants; samples were also taken from regional groups of Presbyterian, Lutheran, Church of Christ, Evangelical Covenant, and Episcopal youth to round out a fair sampling. Girls outnumber boys in a ratio of 54% to 46%, and sophomores slightly outnumber the other three high-school grades, but neither sex nor grade is markedly out of proportion (25% freshmen, 27% sophomores, 26% juniors, 22% seniors). A description of how each denomination is represented in the ecumenical sample (n = 7,050) is found on page 155. Four more parallel national samples (n = 3,934), Lutheran, Covenant, Mennonite, and Orthodox Church of America, supply additional information.

Special efforts were made to include minority groups, residents of inner-city areas, and nonattending church youth. Though one is never 100% successful in recruiting participants, at least three out of four on membership rolls did cooperate—a better batting average than most surveys can report.

Were our participants honest in their self-reports? Or did they press for a halo effect, saying what they think religious people want to hear?

Though pretense is always an issue, we found that a pledge of confidentiality ("only a computer will see your answers") plus a group-administered test situation did encourage a sense of ano-

nymity. Our checks on frankness lead us to believe our participants spoke with candor.

Are Church Youth Different?

Some people assume that church youth are very different from
their peers. The director of one large foundation calls them the
"good kids who have no problems." Some prominent businessmen
refer to them as the rear guard of today's youth, a reflection of the
past.

More myths are circulated about church youth than the facts
support. In fact, to apply any one label to all church youth is
impossible; our study shows them to be remarkably, refreshingly
diverse.

If we are determined to compare church youth and the non-
churched, we can draw some information from the study itself.
Within the sample are: (1) 811 who rarely or never attend church
and 6,239 who sometimes or often do, and (2) 732 whose parents
belong to no church and 6,088 whose parents do.

Comparison of these groups tells us that church and nonchurch
youth are alike in their reactions to common adolescent problems
such as lack of parental understanding, dating problems, lack of
self-confidence, academic problems, and classroom relationships.

It also reveals considerable similarity in political and/or social
attitudes although church youth are probably less conservative politically and less willing to preserve the *status quo* than other
Americans. One can expect more church youth to favor progressive political action and to protest obvious dishonesties.[3]

Church youth are probably more people-oriented. In their attitudes toward the poor and minorities they resemble college
students, ages nineteen to twenty-four, the most liberal group
among youth.

If church youth are in any way a unique subculture, it is in their
beliefs and values. Church youth and those outside the community
of faith differ sharply in: sense of moral responsibility; desire for a
meaningful life; religious participation; social action; self-regard;

feeling for people; God-awareness; and a positive orientation toward the congregation, youth group, and family.

Solid evidence tells us that church youth identify more with their parents; more of them say they have values, attitudes, and life qualities that are the same as those of their parents. In 1968 three out of five American youth saw themselves as different from their parents, whereas only about half the youth of one typical denomination in 1970 claimed this difference. Our data reveal that youth's evaluation of family relationships varies little between denominations.

With contrasts in beliefs and values come contrasts in life-style. The lower incidence of premarital sex, drinking, and drug usage among youth of the church compared with that of the nonchurch group shows an ability or willingness to delay gratification that is related to what church youth value and believe; a personal faith in Jesus Christ makes a great difference in life-style and outlook on life. (See footnote 3 for additional information on the families, schools, and activities of youth in the sample).

What Is the Useful Life of This Study?

Anyone who works with youth knows that times are changing, that "they didn't do it that way when I was young." This awareness poses questions: Are today's youth radically different from youngsters of ten years ago, twenty years ago? Ten or fifteen years from now will there be similar differences?

The answer to these queries is yes if changing fads and moods are one's index, but no if one looks beneath the surface of change. Values, beliefs, attitudes, and concerns are remarkably consistent, irrespective of time, culture, or location. Low self-esteem troubles youth of the Orient just as it does those in America; it crops up in diaries of youth from the fourth, sixteenth, and twentieth centuries. The twenty-five characteristics listed earlier are not unique to any one culture or period.

When an older version of the Youth Research Survey was translated into the Batak language for a study of students at Nommensen University (Indonesia) in 1966, only 7 of the 520 items then in use were considered inappropriate to that culture. Though the students were involved in the revolutionary activity of unseating Sukarno from his throne and radically changing the political situation, their reported concerns, values, beliefs, and feelings were similar to those of students in American church colleges.

There *are* changes today, obvious ones, but their importance has been overstressed in relation to the unchanging dynamics of behavior. Certain universal characteristics, patterns of behavior, and ways of looking at life continue to typify the adolescent and tell *why* he acts as he does. Knowledge of these dynamics can counterbalance our preoccupation with *how* youth are behaving.

There are those who hold that the unprecedented events of the '60s prove that we are seeing a new breed. Anthropologist Margaret Mead contends that events between 1950 and 1970 have irrevocably altered relationships and ushered in a new age. She believes that between generations has occurred a break which is planetary, universal, and new to history. Everyone born and bred before World War II, she says, is an immigrant in time who cannot know what his children experientially know.

Using a national sample of church people, we tested Mead's theory[4] and failed to find the radical break she claims. Using fifty-two scales that measure differences at two-year intervals for a population varying in age between fifteen and sixty-five, we found no differences on two-fifths of the measures. Of the remaining three-fifths, the extreme variation in degree and location of tension between age generations makes it evident that tension (let alone an open break) is pertinent only to certain characteristics. At best the "new breed" theory applies to a small subculture of high-school or college students; at worst, it is another stereotype that does not fit the majority of American youth.

Our evidence leads to the conclusion that any relational gap between youth and parents is the same one which older adults knew as young people.

Are the cries of youth described in this book unique to this day? If intensity of outcry is the issue, then we might say yes. Today's youth seem to know more anxiety than those of former years and seem to have more freedom to speak their minds.

But if the substance is the issue, then I would say no. In my opinion, the five cries described in this book are universal and timeless expressions of need or values: they are the ways in which all youth are alike.

I yell inside my empty cave and my answer is an echo, an echo of cold words and cold pain.

Habel

2   Cry of Self-Hatred

This chapter describes the unvoiced cry that seriously haunts the lives of one young person in five. It rises out of feelings of worthlessness, self-criticism, and loneliness.

The cry of low self-esteem, plaintive and often irritating, is not always easy to understand. We notice a person acting as though he considers himself the most important person in the group. We sense a certain phoniness in his behavior, but fail to recognize the feelings of inadequacy which prompt his look-at-me actions.

Fostering self-esteem is an important goal for home and church. Given a congenial atmosphere and reaffirming adults, youth can change their self-perceptions and gain a new outlook on life. The awareness that one is loved by God and man can be encouraged.

John seems a quiet, shy young man, all eyeglasses and floppy blond hair, sitting in the tenor section of the church choir. He excites neither trouble nor interest for the people around him. His infrequent talk is usually about sports events. It is extremely important to him that his team should win; a loss by his school's team, or his state university, or his favorite professional team can make him morose and depressed for days. Not precisely unfriendly, he seldom opens a conversation; and when he responds to someone else's remarks, he talks a bit too loudly, a bit too fast, as though people might not hear him out unless he gets it all said in a rush of words.

John is a victim of strong feelings of worthlessness. Guilt, anxiety, and loneliness plague him constantly. He is given to erotic

12

fantasies and frequent daydreams, as a way of living out his desires of being a hero. Guilt over masturbation results in a tendency to downgrade himself severely. He is usually a loner, unwilling to force his company on others, sure that he is unworthy of their attention. But when he is with others, he tries hard to please or amuse them; their favorable attention, or their laughter, is of great value to him. Seeing himself as a loser, he identifies with athletic teams and depends on them for a vicarious sense of victory and his own temporary importance.

Wherever he goes, John constantly and silently cries out, "I'm worthless!" The great, urgent need of his life is to be someone he himself could love and respect.

Self-esteem, "feeling good about oneself," is a vital element in a person's life. When it is lacking, alienating and self-destructive types of behavior appear. When it is present, life takes on excitement and purpose.

A person with a sense of worth does more than accept his strengths and weaknesses. He also reflects patient hope and quiet conviction that he will grow and improve. Though he may criticize himself, it is without condemnation; though he may admit limitations, it is without feeling inadequate. Because he feels good about himself, he is free to become involved in meeting the needs of others.

There are few sufferings equal to the pain of feeling no good, unattractive, inadequate, worthless. Kind words spoken to John, for instance, are immediately discounted. "You're just trying to make me feel good." He is prevented from reaching out to others for companionship; he is sure nobody wants him around. "Who'd want me to come to the party? Who'd want me to join the team? Who'd want me to call them up?" Constantly and consistently, John and others like him cut themselves off from the healing qualities of the everyday human associations that persons who have a sense of worth enjoy and take for granted.

The feeling of worthlessness often makes a person turn on himself in anger. Then the cry becomes a mixture of worthlessness, self-hatred, and loneliness. As the most commonly voiced and the most intensely felt of the five cries, it is the first to be discussed.

Three Self-Relational Characteristics
(Personal Faults, Lack of Self-Confidence, Low Estimate of Worth)

Feelings begin in the brain, in a person's perceptions. A patient worried sick over the possibility of a malignancy is suddenly relieved and exuberant when the doctor tells him the lump is benign. A change in perception brings a change in feelings.

Perceptions held over a period of time tend to harden into a fairly persistent combination of reactions or tendencies. To know a person's tendencies is to understand how he will respond to himself, to others, and to life itself. We say, "You better be careful how you talk to him. He has a tendency to be easily hurt." Or, "He has a tendency to think nobody likes him."

Of the many tendencies or dispositions that characterize human beings, the most powerful are the self-relational which have to do with one's feelings about himself. More than any other, these touch the innards of a person's emotional life and spark the glands and the smooth muscles of the autonomic nervous system. When feelings of self-criticism, lack of self-confidence, and low self-worth pummel a person long and hard, they leave their mark on his physical well-being and effective functioning. Often this involves skin disorders, physical ailments, or debilitating psychological states; linked also are drug abuse, suicide, and self-defeating behavior.

What did we find in our study that helps to understand this first cry? We found eight feelings and concerns clustered together to form a constellation of characteristics. Three are feelings about oneself (self-relational), and five are concerns about others (other-relational). They intertwine with sufficient intensity to qualify as a distinct area of need.

The interrelationship of the three self-relational characteristics is shown in the upper part of figure 1.

Distress over personal faults (self-criticism) and lack of self-confidence (personal anxiety) undermine feelings of self-regard: as self-criticism and anxiety mount, self-regard drops lower and lower.

characteristics of
that worthless feeling

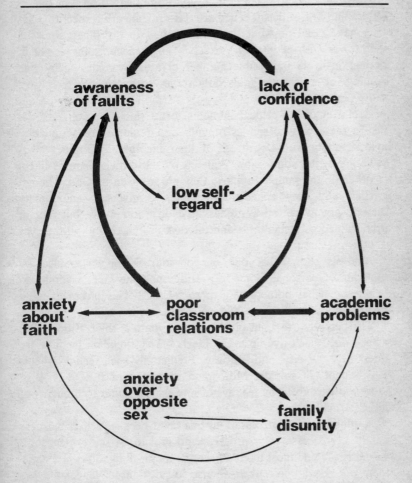

Heaviness of arrow indicates strength of intercorrelation.

Distress over Personal Faults

The big brother in this first constellation of characteristics is distress over personal faults.

A significant portion of church youth are dogged by thoughts of failure and self-criticism. They are self-critical with respect to what they have done or what they have failed to do. They compare themselves with people who excel in an area appealing to them; perfection in an impossible number of areas becomes their goal. Aiming for unrealistic goals only serves to exaggerate their own shortcomings.

A cluster of self-critical thoughts forms this strong characteristic. In these youth, feelings of guilt and remorse are abundantly evident along with awareness of their inability to forgive themselves. Yet, the youth most troubled by self-criticism are as likely as others in the sample to affirm they are forgiven by God. Though intellectually they acknowledge God's forgiveness, emotionally they do not live in an awareness of God's acceptance but remain preoccupied with standards and the task of "making it" in the eyes of others.

Analysis shows that one out of four is much troubled by thoughts of personal blame. An additional one in two admits to being somewhat bothered by these feelings. This is an affliction known, in varying degrees, by most youth.

The persistent thought of self-critical youth is this: "I don't like what I do; I can't live up to my ideals." The attendant feelings are insecurity, self-pity, and jealousy. Predictably such feelings generate thoughts of suicide. More than three out of five (62%) of those *most* troubled by feelings of low esteem admit to thoughts of self-destruction.[1]

A qualifier seems necessary at this point because self-criticism is admittedly necessary for progress and growth. A self-critical individual is the one most likely to see his moral obligations and carry them out. He is most likely to rise to positions of leadership because he can see what is lacking and what needs to be improved in both himself and others. The issue is the *degree* of self-criticism operating in the individual.

Most adolescents go through periods of feeling quite worthless, especially following some disappointing experience in their friendships or having failed to measure up to others in school grades or sports activities. Such feelings usually pass over like clouds. If they persist and dominate, they become destructive because excessive self-criticism tears down self-esteem and interferes with relationships.

Such youth especially need to experience the acceptance and love of others. An atmosphere of mutual acceptance can free them to deal with their negative perceptions and feelings of personal guilt.

Lack of Self-Confidence

Jean quit her Bible discussion group, and no one knew why. Though very shy, she had seemed interested. Later, she admitted, "I quit because class makes me angry—angry with myself. I wanted to take part in the discussion, but I didn't dare." Jean added that she was afraid that anything she said would sound trite or ridiculous, that she was not comfortable just sitting there. "I was afraid someone would call on me and smoke me out. It angers me that I cannot think of anything to say like the rest."

Lack of self-confidence is a top-ranking characteristic in feelings of worthlessness. It is living with the nagging fear, "I'm going to blow it. I'll pull a boner, and everyone will laugh at me." Unchecked, the fear goes a step further and actually inhibits the flow of ideas. If called on to express an opinion, Jean knows her mind will dart frantically around and find nothing to say. This frightening prospect is enough to stop the timid from coming to discussion meetings.

Three out of four of our respondents (74%) are bothered in some degree by feelings of personal anxiety. Only one in four is relatively free of them. The greatest threats are posed by class recitations or activities where one can be humiliated or seen as a failure. Because these youth are thin-skinned and upset by adverse criticism, they fear making mistakes or being seen as "getting out of line." It is hard to overstate their embarrassment over a gurgling stomach, a mispronounced word, or a note that is warbled off-key.

They are convinced they lack talent and realize their dependence on the praise of others. Even as they "bow and scrape," they are bothered by the knowledge of it.

Youth lacking self-confidence screen out activities where they might fail. They won't try out for the school play, work on an important committee, or join in a spontaneous game of volleyball or softball. At a party they'll decline the new game or dance. "Oh, no," they will protest. "I'm no good at that kind of stuff. I couldn't do that."

Discounting their ability without even a trial, such young people cut themselves off not only from the fun of an activity, but also from the possibility for personal growth.

The correlation between Lack of Self-Confidence and Personal Faults (i.e., the degree to which they covary) is high ($r = .73$). In all probability, the two feelings interact reciprocally to increase each other. One who is harsh in his self-criticism usually assumes that others are judging him in the same way. Therefore he tends to be uneasy in group situations and carefully guarded lest he be viewed negatively. This self-consciousness in turn becomes the basis for another round of self-criticism. The person regretfully notes how easily others are able to speak and is angered by his own cloddishness and lack of verbal grace. A college freshman expressed the fear of ridicule and humiliation which underlie a lack of confidence:

> I wish
> That I could
> say what
> I wish
> so that you
> would not laugh
> at me.

> And you say you would
> not laugh
> out loud
> but inside you would
> be laughing

so loud
that I could hear
it from there, too.
So I will remain
quiet
exposing my wishes only
to this paper
which cannot laugh.

Sabine

In 1965 Dr. Morris Rosenberg reported a prize-winning study of 5,042 adolescents in the state of New York, showing the close relationship between low self-confidence and anxiety. According to Rosenberg, an adolescent suffering from pangs of self-contempt may: (1) retreat into the world of imagination where he can dream of himself as worthy, or (2) put up a false front to others to convince them that he is worthy. Both responses tend to separate the person from others.

Other dynamics may also be involved. An adolescent caught in these feelings may concentrate on being very good in order to be loved, on being strong in order to be admired, or on being capable in order to be praised. Standards, rules, and regulations may become too important as measures of worth or achievement. The youngster believes that he is liked not for what he *is* but for the good things he *does*, thus the more he achieves, the more others will like him. Instead of moving toward greater self-expression and self-realization, he sees self-effacement as goodness, and withdrawal from threat as freedom.

Low Self-Regard

The third characteristic is perceiving oneself as a person of low worth, a person without importance.

About one-half of our respondents admit to this perception. Of these, 15% say their perception has become a continuous pattern of reactions. They tend to feel lonely, uncomfortable about the future, and bored with life; they speak about competence, talent, and ability as qualities which others, not they, possess.

An inevitable result of low self-regard is loneliness. A young person with a negative view of himself does not enjoy being alone; he succumbs to thoughts such as these: "I'm not fit to be with. But I have to be with myself. There's no way I can get away. Maybe if I am with other people, it will help take my mind off me. But how can I be with people? They don't want me. I'm not fit to be with."

Few of the lonely see life as a celebration. Most seek anonymity through adopting a public pose and keeping people at arm's length. The jovial heavyweight who joshes about her obesity confesses in private that her joking is a cover-up. She is really a lonely person.

Table 1 indicates the influence of loneliness on personal estimates of life.

TABLE 1
Influence of Loneliness

| Item | Percentage Answering Yes | | |
	Lonely N = 1,305	Sometimes Lonely N = 2,844	Not Lonely N = 2,854
I find life exciting and full of fun.	30	49	68
I feel that my future is in good hands.	32	48	68
I feel no one knows me.	64	37	27

The big issue for most lonely youth is having friends. Most (87%) say that outside their families they really belong to no group and are bothered to some degree by the lack of friends at school (versus 55% of the nonlonely).

It is interesting that most lonely youth report having *some* close friends. Sixteen percent report as many as ten close friends "who really care" about them. Apparently loneliness is not cured by company, nor does solitude necessarily increase it. Aloneness is more than physical separation in life; it is akin to the fear of nonbeing or meaninglessness so often identified with the alienation of the twentieth century, which Kierkegaard believed was cured only through an identification with God.

The issue is not so much friends, as the ability to commit oneself to another. To know the trust of deep attachments a young person must entrust himself to others. Inability to do so robs him of the affection which he needs so desperately. Unable to open his life to others in a caring and loving way, he does not experience the love and affection of others which could give him a sense of well-being and worth.

Nancy expressed it well:

> Standing apart
> I heard you say hello
> it was sweet of you to try
> but I was (after all)
> standing apart.
> > Nancy Nelson, age seventeen

Five Other-Relational Characteristics

Low self-esteem inhibits relationships, and poor human relationships erode self-esteem. Attitudes toward the opposite sex, academic problems, parents, and God affect and are affected by self-perception. Figure 1 shows how these additional five characteristics interrelate with the first three.

Classroom Relationships

Most church youth find school relationships bothersome to some degree. They feel critical of insensitive classmates and unsympathetic teachers. They are bothered by the "pressure to do what others do" and are disappointed by the way they succumb ("I often act different from what I really am"). See table 2.

Academic Problems

Many educators oppose the use of grades in evaluating academic performance because of their impact on the self-esteem and motivation of young people.

To what extent do low grades increase youth's feelings of low self-esteem? Our data show that students who get low grades, who

TABLE 2

Concern over Classroom Relationships among Church Youth

Ecumenical Sample

(N = 7,050)

Classroom Relationships

Item	Percentage Concerned*
Classmates at school could be more friendly.	53
In a group I often act different from what I really am.	52
Some classmates are inconsiderate of my feelings.	51
There are cliques (closed groups) in my school.	51
I feel pressure at school to do what others do.	50
There are not enough opportunities to be with a mixed group (boys and girls) in social activities.	41
Some teachers are sarcastic and critical of what I do.	38
Some of my teachers do not understand me.	37
My interests are often different from those of others my age.	35

* Very Much, Quite a Bit, Somewhat

are unable to concentrate on their school work, and who worry about their academic performance usually rank low in self-esteem. Lack of competence, skill, or application in academic matters is linked with a low self-image. One can speculate in several directions:

1. Teachers' evaluations (grades) lower or raise a student's self-esteem; or
2. Feelings of low esteem lead to the fantasying and daydreaming that prevent concentration—with resulting lower grades; or
3. Less academically able youth are more troubled with low self-esteem whether they are in school or not.

Though our data show that low grades bother recipients more than most adults suppose, low grades are not a major cause of low self-esteem. If grades were not given at school, it is likely that a youth troubled by low estimate of self would continue to feel worthless. Other comparisons would still lead him to say, "I am not as smart as others my age."

Abrasive parent-youth relationships also influence grades. Youth with low grades report more conflicts at home and express more concern over their parents' relationship with each other.

Our data show differences in the life-style of academic low-achievers which bear a strong relation to grades (see table 3).

TABLE 3
Percentage Saying Yes to Questionable Activities

Item	Grades in School				
	Very Low N = 157	Below Avg. N = 456	Avg. N = 2,564	Above Avg. N = 2,904	Excell. N = 761
I have taken things which did not belong to me.	75	68	57	48	41
I sometimes get "high" on alcoholic beverages.	61	45	35	26	22
Sexual intercourse on a date (is an option).	33	18	16	11	11
Use of drugs (is an issue).	36	20	12	9	7

Differences in values and socioeconomic level are associated, too, with grade differences. Thirty-eight percent of youth with excellent grades had fathers in a profession and college-educated mothers, as compared to 14% of youth with low grades.

It is evident that factors other than native ability are linked to academic achievement, and factors other than grades, with low self-esteem.

Anxiety about God-Relationship

Low self-regard is related to anxiety about one's faith and to a troubled awareness of distance and alienation from God. Whether experienced as spiritual lonesomeness, inability to live up to one's religious convictions, or a concern over life after death, anxiety over the God-relationship characterizes low self-esteem youth.

Ten years ago, in a study of church youth, *Profiles of Church Youth* (1963), I found a correlation ($r = .49$) between the dimensions, Feelings of Inadequacy and God-Relationship. In 1972, using different youth populations, the same dimensions emerged with a similar correlation ($r = .40$). Apparently, youth with low self-esteem are anxious about all of life's realities.

How a sense of alienation includes the God-relationship is indicated by the percentage of friendless youth who cannot believe in a personal, caring God (see table 4).

TABLE 4
Percentage Saying Yes to Faith Items

| | Number of Friends | |
Item	None N = 359	10 or More N = 1,769
Jesus is the divine Son of God.	44	72
God cares for me in a special way.	45	75
I have a sense that my prayers have been answered by God.	40	70

In another study Peter Benson and Bernard Spilka found a fairly high association ($r = .46$) between self-esteem and viewing God as a loving and accepting person. Youth of low self-esteem tend to see God as vindictive and controlling. Apparently, their inner needs call for a more rejecting God who punishes rather than loves the evildoer.[2]

Concern over Family Relationships

Rosenberg, in his study of self-esteem, gave special attention to the effect of parental disinterest. He focused upon parents' knowledge of children's friends, interest in their child's report cards, and degree to which the young person participates in dinner conversations. He concluded with this statement:

Whether one belongs to the upper, upper-middle, lower-middle, or lower social classes; whether one is a Protestant, Catholic, or Jew; whether one is male or female; whether one lives in a large city, a medium sized community, or small town—whichever of these conditions obtain, the result is essentially the same: if the parent manifests indifference to the child, that child is less likely to have a high level of self-regard.

He also found that low self-esteem was likelier if a mother were indifferent to low grades than if she nagged about them. In other words, the most telling comment of low self-esteem youth with respect to parents was, "She seldom commented on my work."

Overstrictness is also associated with low self-perception. Kirkpatrick has a theory that parents who feel inferior are sensitive to their modest achievements and limited importance in the scheme of things. When children fail to obey or show proper respect for their authority, it is seen as another sign of their own failure and calls up strong emotions. Cockiness in the child begets a strict, punitive reaction in the parent who sees it not as a compensation for inferiority feelings, but as a threat to his authority (Sebald 1968). Such parents may also be preoccupied with standards; because they cannot accept themselves, they have unrealistic expectations for themselves and their children.

Since overstrictness is reported by two out of five church young people, one can speculate that large numbers of parents are insecure, rule-oriented people. Overcontrolling and overprotective, they serve as models for their children, while tending to pass on their own low self-esteem. A local congregational ministry must take seriously the low self-esteem of parents.

Relationship with Opposite Sex

Most youth worry about relating successfully to members of the opposite sex and eventually finding the right person for a happy marriage. To have dates is for many a measure of worth. Fifty-one percent of church youth spent time every day (or quite often) thinking about "how to keep boys/girls interested in me." Almost half (47%) spent time every day (or quite often) wondering "whether or not I will find a life partner." Concern over finding a life partner correlates with two major indicants of low self-esteem, namely, Personal Faults ($r = .49$) and Lack of Self-Confidence ($r = .40$). These correlations are highly significant in light of the importance dating holds for many youth.

We have described youth's feelings of worthlessness and have shown how they reach into all relationships, creating a kind of cosmic alienation.

The hopeful thesis of this analysis is that friends, teachers, parents, and God can establish a quality of relationship that enhances feelings of esteem, changes the way of perceiving the self, and helps young people to believe in their worth and significance.

This is what the gospel seeks to do—to convince a person that he is loved by God and is an important member of God's family. When such a message dawns on a person who feels worthless, it is "good news" indeed. His change in perception leads to a new outlook on life; he emerges from the cave of loneliness and comes back into touch with himself, others, and God.

How many youth are we talking about who have a special need for such a ministry?

Proportion of Low Self-Esteem Youth

One out of five (20%) of all youth in our survey are buoyed by a sense of positive self-esteem. If we drop one criterion (e.g., high grades), we find that two in five (37%) are relatively free of self-critical attitudes and thoughts of suicide and hold themselves in relatively high self-regard.

On the other hand, tragically, 20% of church youth harbor thoughts of severe self-criticism and even suicide. Among these are 2% whose loss of contact with themselves and others is compounded by alienation from God.

On the average, one out of five church youth enjoys high self-esteem, and one out of five suffers under the heavy hand of self-accusation. For the majority of church youth it is a concern of varying proportions.[3]

It is well to observe that low self-esteem is passed on in families. Anxiety and stress characterize all ages; defensive behavior is not uniquely adolescent. Youth differ primarily in that their emotions are more volatile and their behavior more extreme and less controlled. Practically speaking, a ministry that is effective for youth applies also to their parents.

Youth's Awareness of Their Need

Do low self-esteem youth want to change in the way they relate to themselves, to others, and to God? We offered survey statements which describe opportunities a church might provide (e.g., to learn to make friends and be a friend). Response possibilities were:

1. No—I am not interested in the opportunity.
2. Much—I am very interested and would go out of my way to participate.
3. Some—I am interested but would not make a special effort to participate.

Which of the forty opportunities proved most attractive to the low self-esteem youth drawn from the ecumenical sample? (These are the 572 youth who score high on Personal Faults and Lack of Self-Confidence: low on Self-Regard.)

Their highest preference is a tie (78%): to find meaning in life; to learn how to make friends and be a friend. Second out of forty possibilities are opportunities that involve leaving their public posture and taking off their masks. Three out of four want to be "more of the real me" in a group. They want help in finding friends and learning to be friends to members of both sexes. Friends are to them what bread is to the hungry and clothes to the naked.

What is needed is a ministry of friendship—activities that bring people together to interact.

Three out of four want to be part of a caring, accepting group. Two out of three want a group that, in addition to offering acceptance, also confronts one another with an honest, frank sharing of personal feelings. They want small-group experiences that get at the feeling level and help them to come out from under their public posture.

One opportunity especially singled out by the low-esteem youth (N = 572) was this one: "I would like to find a way to deal with my lack of self-confidence." Next was a related item: "I would like assistance in understanding myself and the reason for my problems." Sixty-one percent declared much interest in "experiencing a closer relationship with God." Table 5 gives dramatic evidence of the kinds of help these youth would like.

TABLE 5

Opportunities Preferred by Low Self-Esteem Youth

N = 572

Item	Percentage Much Interested
Relationship with others	
To learn how to make friends and be a friend.	78
To learn to be more of the real me when I am with other people.	77
To learn to get along better with members of the opposite sex.	75
To experience acceptance in a group of people who really care about each other.	74
Group meetings where people feel free to say what they really think and are honest about what bothers them.	66
To learn how to be a friend to those who are lonely and rejected.	60
Recreation and social activities where youth get acquainted.	58
Relationship with God	
To find meaning and purpose in my life.	78
To experience a closer relationship with God.	61
To find a good basis for deciding what is right and wrong.	60
Relationship with Self	
Assistance in understanding myself and the reasons for my problems	72
To find a way to deal with my lack of self-confidence.	69
To learn to live with the pressures people place on me (friends, school, parents, church, etc.)	64

Another indication of the help they desire comes from the study *Clergy-Youth Counseling Project* funded by the National Institute of Mental Health. Four-hundred high-school juniors in experimental congregations listed changes they wanted for themselves during the fifteen months of the project. Each listed two to five hoped-for changes.

A striking feature of this list is the high interest in bettering one's relationship with others, with God, and with oneself. The youth who described these three dimensions are typical and were not ones singled out because of low self-esteem. It seems that self-esteem and enhanced relationships are goals welcomed by most church youth.

TABLE 6
Hoped-for Changes of 400 Youth

Hoped-for Changes	No. Times Mentioned by 400 Youth
Better relationships	681
Be a better Christian	318
Have better self-concept	276
Have more self-confidence	256
Do better in school	220
Be a better person	206
Overcome personal faults	192
Improved parent/family relationships	123
More involved in church	75
Better physical appearance	73
Improved personality	67

In what direction does a parent or youth leader go to meet the needs which are overwhelmingly apparent?

An Appropriate Approach

The hope of the Christian church is that all men might love God, their neighbor, and themselves. Christ showed how these relationships intertwine when he said we are to love our neighbor as ourselves. The Apostle John added, "We love because he first loved us." Love begets love.

Through his incarnation and life, Christ showed that God's message is communicated by showing it, living it, speaking it. It is a Living Word that is to be heard, seen, felt, and experienced through another person. The essence of the message is what a little girl left in a note to her dad: "I love you—is that okay?"

The message, which people are to incarnate, centers in promise and possibilities: no person is a hopeless case. Possibilities for change are open to everyone because implicit in each of God's promises are the words, "I am with you." The unique potential in a Christian ministry is the awareness of God working in man, inspiring both the will and the deed.

A Christian youth ministry should be an extension of one's theology. The accent should be not on problem-solving (overcoming fears, gaining confidence, improving one's self-concept), but on helping youth to become aware of possibilities found in a relationship with Jesus Christ. This means communicating to youth that they are loved, are important, have potential, and can look forward to growth and positive change. A change in their awareness will not come through indoctrination or the repetition of words, but through the "living words" of people who embody God's message. These hope-inspiring people, like little Christs, are convinced there is hope for every person and that God's yes applies to everyone.

An incarnational theology and a sensitivity to low self-esteem youth lead to these warnings:

1. Obligations, expectations, and rules should be deemphasized in the way adults work with youth and in the content of their discussions. Low self-esteem people are constantly saying no about themselves. They do not need a louder negative voice.
2. A rules-oriented religion—which low self-esteem youth tend to accept—must be exposed as practical atheism by contrasting it with a gospel of affirmation.
3. The techniques of hearty encouragement, bushels of compliments, and a series of social gatherings are not enough. Low self-esteem youth need a community or small group where they can live in the awareness of being accepted.
4. Competitive activities (e.g., "head-trip" discussions or competitive sports) tend to encourage unfavorable comparisons and threaten the more anxious youth. Socializing activities should stress cooperative activities where no one loses and discussions where no one is seen as wrong.

Concern and Warmth Are Key Factors

A ministry (whether in home or church) which works toward greater self-esteem among youth and adults must create the conditions that are freeing and disarming to low self-esteem people. It must accent warmth and congeniality to counteract the chilling effects of an anxious and self-condemning spirit.

What is needed most are people who have found an identity in life and are willing to share themselves with others. The primary qualifications for such adults center in what they incarnate and believe, in being sensitive to others and open to their possibilities. They must be people who can step into another person's shoes and just as easily step back into their own.

The important factor in helping another person to esteem and a sense of identity is not problem-solving techniques or expertise. It is the empathic and warm relationship of a concerned person. In a sense, the words said or specific relating techniques used matter little, so long as the interaction establishes a warm relationship.

If the essentials in helping youth to a sense of personal significance are the human qualities of empathy, warmth, and genuineness, then untrained people, both youth and adults, can be helpful.

Elements Working for Self-Esteem

A climate of warmth encourages self-esteem in several ways. First, it frees the person to verbalize his feelings and to put into words the emotions churning inside. Once in words, feelings can be dealt with rationally; the person can be guided by good sense and sound judgment, instead of irrational drives.

Second, a congenial affirming climate encourages one to accept new information about himself, to hear God's promise, and to accept and acknowledge strengths and weaknesses. In hearing and experiencing love and acceptance, self-perception changes.

It is hard to overstate the importance of times when youth and adults can acknowledge their humanity through sharing honest doubts and irrational fears. There is a quiet release and growth as masks are removed and one finds acceptance and love. What must be fought in home and church is the attitude "You shouldn't talk like that" which drives emotions underground to continue their eroding effect on the human spirit.

We cannot solve youth's problems or manipulate their growth; we can only provide conditions for growth—the warmth of caring spirits, inquiring minds, and awareness of God's message.

Effects of Mutual Interchange

Does mutuality really make a discernible difference in the lives of youth?

Some evidence is available from the *Clergy-Youth Counseling Project* referred to earlier.

Youth of forty congregations in the Minneapolis-St. Paul area participated in a two-year study designed to test the effect of non-professionals interacting with youth. Young people in twenty congregations served as Controls, and a second group from twenty randomly assigned congregations served as Experimentals. All took the Youth Research Survey at the beginning, middle, and end of the project. The difference was that the Experimentals had the choice of conversing with their pastors about their counseling profiles; congregational youth leaders had the stimulus of a group report on their youth and the encouragement to try out new ways to meet some of their expressed needs; parents in some of the experimental congregations enrolled in Parent Effectiveness Training[4] and learned how to relate better to their youth. These opportunities were optional and integrated into the normal program of the twenty Experimental congregations. No one was asked to counsel a fixed number of times or to participate in any of the congregational activities.

Distress over personal faults and lack of self-confidence, academic problems, and classroom relationships dropped significantly among the experimental youth. Their gain in these aspects of self-esteem stood in contrast with youth in the control congregations.

Clearly, increased adult interest and attention make a measurable impact on the lives of youth.

My dad and I don't get along too
good the past couple of years. That's
why I'm out goofin' around tonight.
I think I'm afraid of my parents,
kinda, inside.

A seventeen-year-old boy

3   Cry of Psychological Orphans

The most poignant cry is the sob of despair or shriek of sheer
frustration among youth living in atmospheres of parental hatred
and distrust. Often it ends in running away from home, delinquent
behavior, suicide, or other self-destructive behavior. This chapter
identifies the four major characteristics of such homes: family
pressures; distress over relationships with parents; disappointment
in family unity; and a negative perception of one's family social
concerns. Because youth despairing over their family situation
often think of suicide, we will also give consideration to this third
highest killer of youth. The chapter ends with a section that briefly
reviews elements which make for family health.

In Robert Frost's poem "The Death of the Hired Man," two
characters each try to define the word *home*. Warren defines it as a
kind of mechanical necessity, without warmth or kindness:

> Home is the place where, when you have to go there,
> They have to take you in.

Mary, on the other hand, sees home as something akin to an
earthly expression of God's grace:

> I should have called it
> Something you somehow haven't to deserve.

There are homes of both kinds on every street and others with all the gradations between. Young people go in and out of them every day and experience the powerful effect of their family's atmosphere.

This second of the five cries of youth (Self-Hatred, Psychological Orphans, Social Protest, Prejudice, Joy) rises from young people who desperately need the stability, support, and love of a home they don't have to deserve. The cry of these young people is, "I need to be part of a family where we love and accept and care about each other."

The young people of this chapter can be predictably placed in only one category: a troubled home situation. To any question relating to family, they tend to give a negative response.

They answer as youth *whose preoccupation is their distressing family situation.* No other characteristics join this constellation— not even those related to self-esteem or religious faith; neither self-deprecation nor religious disinterest is uniquely found among these youth. Except for home life, they are typical church youth. There is nothing in what they believe, value, think, or do that points a blaming finger at them for disruption in the home. It is probably the parents who are primarily responsible.

The need for help is so intense for some that, lacking the encouragement of adult friends and support groups, they may turn to irrational and tragic actions. One example is suicide; another is rebellious or delinquent behavior; yet another is running away to join some group whose life-style is part of the counterculture.

The distress of problems centering in the family is illustrated by skin-resistance data. Disturbed adolescents whose problems tend to center at home in active family conflict show greater skin reactivity than adolescents whose difficulties center outside the home. The feelings generated by tension between parents and siblings is so intense that the body registers the impact (Goldstein et al. 1970).

This chapter draws attention to psychological orphans who lack the support and love needed for healthy development and identifies what may be needed in a ministry to these youth. Survey information will describe what racks the emotions of about one church youth in five.

characteristics of
youth in family conflict

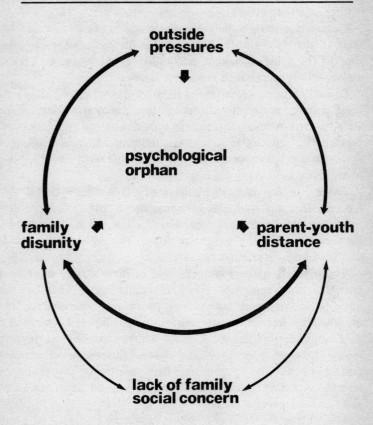

outside
pressures

psychological
orphan

family
disunity

parent-youth
distance

lack of family
social concern

Heaviness of arrow indicates strength of intercorrelation.

Family Pressures

About 21% of our respondents have known separation or divorce of parents, illness, financial duress, parent-youth strife, absenteeism of the father, and serious difficulties due to such calamities as unemployment and death. In some cases, pressures have piled up and the family suffers under the cumulative impact of several unsettling events or conditions.

Disturbance in the family negatively affects personality development of the child who is dependent on his parents for emotional support for living, behaving, and thinking. We can take a closer look at some events which pressure a family.

Divorce/separation. No more than 8% report divorced or separated parents; apparently divorce is less common among families affiliated with religious institutions than among the population as a whole (25% in 1960). A faith commitment and/or an identification with a religious community is associated with lower incident of divorce.

Among the 8% isolated by this study, it is evident that divorce has created many problems for some and relatively few problems for others. We can make generalizations based on comparisons between the 8% who have experienced divorce in their families and the remaining youth in the sample.

Youth whose parents are separated or divorced are more bothered than the average over lack of family unity. They are also more likely to report other family pressures. Interestingly, they do not differ from all other youth in being troubled over lack of parental understanding or lack of self-confidence and personal faults. However, a third measure shows a lower estimate of worth among youth living in families where divorce or separation has become necessary. Also, these young people do have more difficulty with their school studies.

The staying power of a religious faith may be indicated by the fact that fewer divorced parents than nondivorced parents are members of a church (55% versus 82%). Paralleling the less frequent church membership of divorced parents is a lower religious interest among their children when compared with all other church youth. Their lessened religious interest shows up in a variety of ways. Fewer youth of divorced parents (than of nondivorced parents) are interested in help from their church or participate actively in the life of their congregation. Fewer are charitable toward people commonly condemned or feel a sense of moral responsibility. Fewer are conscious of a personal, caring God or report that their families go out of their way to help others.

These differences, though larger than can be credited to chance, cannot be considered major problems contributing to family conflict. The research data make it evident that though divorce is for some a tragic event, for others it leaves few emotional bruises.

Rosenberg's 1967 study shows some of the variable effects of divorce. For instance, a marital rupture has far less effect if the mother is older, is a Protestant, and does not remarry. The greatest strain occurs when the divorced mother is young and when her child is very young. But when the effects of such divorces are averaged with those for whom divorce has had little effect, the average negative impact is sharply reduced. A 1971 study of 1,566 divorced parents found that the detrimental effects of divorce were not as devasting as often assumed (Burchinal 1971).

In this study of church youth, divorce emerges as one of many factors that disturb the families of youth. Because divorce is clearly understood, it will be used as a basis for comparison with other factors more disturbing to youth.

Family difficulties. Unfortunate as divorce may be, more discernible tension is associated with difficulties posed by prolonged illness, unemployment, death or injuries, or personal problems. Youth living under such pressures are more troubled with respect to all family relationships. As would be expected, self-regard goes down during crisis times for these youth.

Trouble with father. Though the variables just mentioned are upsetting to youth, an even more sensitive nerve is touched by the statement "I have trouble getting along with my father." Surprising as it may seem to armchair psychologists, difficulties with father are twelve times as likely to predict family disunity as the fact of divorce. A boy who is at odds with his dad is powerfully affected by his conflict situation and prone to condemn himself for it. His self-esteem goes down. Though such a young person is often less religious than other church youth, the differences are not commensurate with the marked contrasts in how he feels about his family and about himself. Not to get along with dad is an emotionally potent variable. If there is conflict, therefore, someone is needed to take dad's place and provide psychological support.

What if the young person has trouble getting along with his mother? A separate analysis of such youth gives almost identical results, except for one addition. An inability to communicate is felt more keenly when mother lacks interest or will not listen. Such an impasse in communication is reported more often by youth who have trouble getting along with their mothers.

Here are some of the most sensitive and frustrating irritations being experienced by youth who have trouble getting along with either parent:

My parents (mother or father) nag me.
My parents (mother or father) try to pry into my private life.
My parents (mother or father) do not like some of my friends.

There is nothing in our survey that suggests a reason for the parent-youth conflict. Nowhere in any of the items of behavior, values, attitudes, or beliefs is there evidence that the youth themselves are posing obstacles to communication. The task appears to be one of moving *parents* closer to their children. The size of the task is indicated by the fact that one in four reports trouble getting along with the father. Of these, nearly half (44%) are also at odds with the mother.

Distress over Parental Relationships

Whereas the first characteristic identifies family pressures, the second describes the young person's feelings about parental relationships. It includes distress over lack of communication and understanding between a youth and his parents, chagrin over feeling treated like a child, and disappointment in his parents' distrust or rejection of him and his friends.

Lack of understanding. The cluster of items forming this characteristic describes parental attitudes and actions that interfere with understanding. From youth's answers to these items, one can draw several conclusions. One-third of church youth are much bothered by their inability to communicate with mother. They find that the frequently used stratagem of either parent is to nag, criticize friends, express suspicions, and give orders. Parents of these youth display a notable lack of understanding and sensitivity about their teenager's feelings. Instead of communicating as one who respects another, they are inclined to do what destroys relationships. They dig into their youth's privacy, as though suspecting the worst, and overcontrol his actions as though the teenager could not be trusted to act responsibly.

By comparison with the teachers and "experts" whom they meet, young people see their parents' way of treating them as ill-informed and ridiculous. Many teenagers doubt their parents' reliability and, in some cases, question their ability to rear children. Parenthood as a "natural right" may be seen as the last stand of the amateur in American society.

The above tongue-in-cheek comment applies especially to youth who suffer under conditions of poor family health, who live with parents not able to cope with life's realities—parents who, in many instances, can be called "living disasters." In many cases they are parents who, out of a mistaken concept of their role, are overstrict and distrustful.

Blocked communication between parents and youth typifies more homes than do shouting matches. It is frequently found in homes where parents are conscientious to a fault but inhibited by a mistaken concept of role. Instead of admitting their humanity and acknowledging their clay feet, they pose as authorities, godlike towers of strength and unfailing judgment. The message that comes through is "I'm okay, but you are not." The reaction of some youth is "Hypocrite."

Too-strict parents. Overregulation of children is a common error of church people. When we divided the sample into groups based on youth's answer to the item "My parents (mother or father) are too strict," we found considerable variation, with about two out of five (39%) bothered very much or quite a bit by overstrictness.

A major irritant in the overstrict home has to do with communication. According to the youth reports, there is little discussion of problems and only telling by the parents. The typical too-strict parent nags and pries and is unwilling to credit youth with the sense to make their own decisions. Teenagers, they assume, must be told what to do.

A second source of distress is the way a too-strict parent relates to his children's friends. The stricter the parent, the less likely he is to approve the friends his child enjoys. Over half (58%) of the youth of the strictest parents report that their friends are neither liked nor approved. They are mystified by their parents' behavior and can't understand why they act as they do. It is as though their parents have forgotten how it feels to be young.

One outcome of extreme strictness is greater tension in the home. No other groups under comparison contrast as sharply in parent-youth relationships as those divided on the basis of parental strictness. Extreme differences in scores appear on measures of family unity and parental understanding.

What happens to the young person? Self-regard tends to be low and self-condemnation high for youth who struggle under the regime of overcontrol. Mingled with these feelings is a longing to get out from under the parental thumb. One-half of overcontrolled youth say that a goal of personal freedom and independence is of "extreme importance" to them.

Another obvious outcome is parent-youth conflict. Life in the home becomes a power struggle: the two members cannot get along because each tries to assert his will over the other. Irritations increase for youth who feel saddled with tyrannical or overcontrolling parents as is shown in figure 3.

It should not be inferred from past comments that the ideal family should operate without controls. Permissiveness may be as ineffective as authoritarian methods. It is under conditions of either extreme that adolescents are most likely to rebel (Kandel and Lesser 1972).

The adolescent needs to be treated as a maturing person—one his parent speaks *with* rather than *to*. He needs a parent who is consistent and firm in discipline while remembering what adoles-

Figure 3

How Irritation with Parents Varies
in Relation to Degree Parents are Perceived as Strict

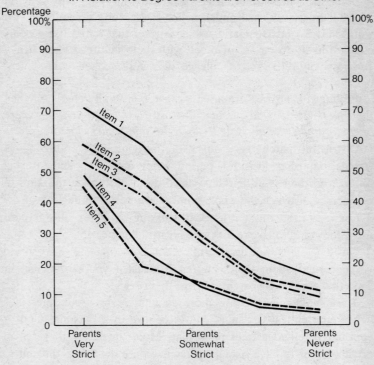

Item 1. My parents (mother or father) nag me.
Item 2. My parents seem to have forgotten how it feels to be young.
Item 3. My parents (mother or father) do not understand my dating problem.
Item 4. My parents (mother or father) do not let me make my own decisions.
Item 5. My parents (mother or father) try to pry into my private life.

cence was like. Trust is the essential element, a two-way street which must involve the child as well as the parent.

Distrustful parents. Some parents hold the pessimistic view that the full bloom of original sin occurs in the teen years. In paranoid fashion, they believe that devilment is afoot requiring alertness for possible chicaneries.

Distrustful and authoritarian parents of this kind impede good parental relationships. Kandel, in his 1972 study of youth in two worlds (U.S. and Denmark), demonstrates that authoritarian parents are likely to be out of touch with their children. Their heavy emphasis on rules and obedience discourages open communication.

Feelings of mistrust are a potent factor in family conflict. When there is concern over parental distrust, *it is nineteen times more likely to predict family disunity than the simple fact of a divorce.*

Distrustful parents are guilty of: nagging, not approving of friends, imposing decisions, prying, being too strict, and pressing religion on their children. They do little to encourage the kind of democracy in which the whole family participates in decision-making or where the children assist in working out rules. On the contrary, they tend to give orders with no attitude of caring.

Our data show that distrustful parents sometimes have reason to be concerned about their children. Untrusted youth often act in ways that cause their parents to trust them even less.

These young people are more susceptible to group pressures concerning ethical decisions. Fewer believe in a personal God or consider a religious faith important. More are likely to get high on alcohol or to have sexual intercourse on a date. It is difficult to tell whether parents sense an inclination toward unacceptable behavior and become distrustful, or whether the youth, sensing distrust, make deliberate decisions to justify their parents' suspicions.

Whether parental distrust or rebellious behavior come first, it is reasonable to say that distrust is a snowball rolling downhill, getting bigger and dirtier as it goes.

Sorenson's 1973 study, *Adolescent Sexuality in Contemporary*

America, adds a helpful dimension. He reports that of all the sexual-behavior groups he studied, sexual adventurers are most in conflict with their parents. Of all sexual adventurers, 58% feel they have never gotten to know their fathers, and 40% believe they have never gotten to know their mothers.

One tragic response to a lack of parental trust is suicide. The percentage who consider self-destruction mounts in direct relation to a youth's feeling of being untrusted. Our data show that, of the untrusted, more have the feeling they will not live long. Fewer see life as exciting, and fewer are hopeful of the future. Self-regard is lowest for youth who feel least trusted by their parents.

Family Disunity

A third characteristic of youth living in troubled homes is their sensitivity to a lack of closeness and oneness of family members. They are bothered by the frigid atmosphere and lack of understanding and consideration for one another; they are disturbed by the poor quality of interaction between parents and children.

Youth idealize a happy family. They often wish the family would enjoy social activities or sports or outings as a family, hoping these events would help bring everyone together.

In the more distressful family situations, the youth are perplexed as well as troubled. They cannot understand why their parents act as they do, why father and mother do not get along as they should, why neither parent shows the interest a young person wants.

Predictors of family disunity. What contributes most to family disunity? What variables are most frequently associated with a tense emotional climate? What are the relative effects on family climate of such variables as parents' occupations, financial duress, illness, divorce, mobility, and the like? How important are variables about which something can be done such as open communication, conflict resolution, trust, right use of authority, and relating to one another?

To find answers, we assessed the degree to which each of thirty-nine variables is related to family disunity. By means of a multi-variate analysis, we identified the irritations most frequently associated with distressed families.

I find it highly significant that sociological variables which are often cited as reasons for the "breakdown of the home" are of little importance. Matters such as socioeconomic level, mother's employment, mobility, or size of family are so minimal in their impact that they can be dismissed from consideration as far as the families of church youth are concerned.

What do emerge in the youth's self-reports are psychological issues. The one that most strongly predicts family disunity is the simple statement "My father and mother do not get along. This bothers me." *It is at least twenty times[1] more powerful a predictor of family disunity than the fact of divorce.* When parents are at odds with each other, youth are most likely to report a fractured or disunited home. This is far and away the most decisive variable in identifying a family that is bleeding and youth who are hurting. Ranking second in predictive power is parental distrust. Unless the parents are helped to make peace with each other and learn what it means to trust, the children will suffer.

Admittedly, comparing parental conflict with divorce is like comparing a high fever with death. One is a current situation, the other is past history. The comparison, however, is valid in pointing up where remedial help is needed.

One boy wrote, "I hope [when married] that I will be stronger emotionally than my parents are. I hope not to fight and cry in front of my kids or be bitchy to them because of my own problems. Kids don't know what they have done when someone turns on them like that, and it hurts every time it happens—even at eighteen years old."

What accounts for the greatest variation in family unity are the issues to which the message and ministry of the Christian church addresses itself: the walls that separate people and alienate one person from another. These sources of dissension are ones about which something *can* be done.

Predictors of family unity. About half (53%) of the population of church youth report accord between their parents; the other half

(47%) admit there are some differences. What makes for greater accord and family unit? Our study singles out these three: *parental accord, parental trust*, and *open communication*.

One in four youth report that their parents not only relate well to each other but also trust their teenage children. Most of these 25% have the added bonus of feeling free to discuss their problems with mother. For the 16% who report the presence of all three positive qualities in their family life, few are in any way bothered by family disunity.[2]

Too Hurt to Help—Lack of Social Concern

A fourth characteristic of families in conflict is a lack of social concern among its members. Troubled youth see their parents as unresponsive to the needs of people outside their home, uninvolved in any form of social action or helping activity.[3]

Most church youth report some social involvement by their families. Two out of three note that their parents care for others and believe their folks would rise to the defense of anyone who is being persecuted or hurt. They appreciate the example their parents set.

A large minority, however, do not see their parents as caring people. More than two in five (44%) admit that their families seldom do anything to help meet social problems and that they do not feel free to invite persons of other races into their homes. A similar percentage (42%) cannot recall any family conversations where they have discussed sharing their money with people in need.

As families become more and more preoccupied with their own conflicts and poor family health, they increasingly resist helping others. Parents who are at each other's throats can turn as quickly to fight racial integration or oppose new housing for senior citizens. The same embittered words that draw blood in the home can be used against others who threaten their security. Such parents should be encouraged to accept marriage counseling, for greater accord in the home and community and, most of all, for the psychological health of their children.

A report of the National Conference on Family Relations concluded that marriage counseling is an inescapable function of the pastor since he maintains standards of marriage, administers the sacraments, is called during family crises, and is involved in the attitudes and responsibilities of the members of the family throughout their total life-span (Morris 1965).

Suicide

Because suicide is so inextricably linked with low self-esteem and family conflict, it seems appropriate now to consider this third leading cause of death in the age group from fifteen to twenty-four years (Schecter and Sternlof 1970). Among persons of college age it is the second leading cause of death, outranked only by accidents (Weddige and Steinhilber 1971).

Suicide is no respecter of social, racial, economic, religious, intellectual, or cultural background, but it does favor age, beginning at fifteen. It marks the end of an unsuccessful struggle to tolerate frustration and despair, to achieve a sense of being, confidence in self, and confidence in being loved.

It was Hall who observed back in 1904 that an almost universal fantasy among children is "If I die, my parents will feel sorry."

Among college students, intellectual competence tends to characterize those who take their lives. A study by Bodin showed that suicides had higher grades than average (grade point averages of 3.18 as opposed to 2.50) and had won a greater proportion of scholastic awards (58% versus 5%). Yet they were filled with doubts about adequacy, dissatisfied with grades, and despondent over their general academic aptitude. It is likely that among the many factors one finds overambitious parents who push them to achieve academically and to excel for the glory of the family.

Suicide and attempted suicide are best seen as the culmination of progressive family disorganization and social maladjustment. The high association of suicide with disrupted families is dramatized by the Cheyenne Indians, whose teenage suicide rate is ten times the national average. Decline in self-esteem and destructive family conflict combine to make thoughts of suicide for the Indian an impelling force (Dizmang 1970).

The motives for suicide in children cannot be understood without considering their family situations.

> In study after study, the home lives of suicidal children have been characterized as disruptive or chaotic. Their histories generally include several of the following indices of family disruption: 1) Frequent moving from one neighborhood or city to another, with many changes of school; 2) family estrangement because of quarreling between parents or between parent(s) and child; 3) great financial difficulties and impoverishment; 4) sibling conflict; 5) illegitimate children; 6) paternal or maternal absence; 7) conflict with stepparent(s); 8) cruelty, rejection, or abandonment by parent(s); 9) institutionalization of adolescent or family member (hospital, jail, reformatory, etc.); 10) suicide attempts by parents; and 11) alcoholic parents.
>
> Such poor family life has been hypothesized to lead to the following conflicts: A fear or knowledge of being unloved; fear of harsh punishment; desire to escape from intolerable conditions; lack of meaningful relationships, creation of guilt; spite; depression; loneliness; hostility; conflict; anxiety; and other affective states, any of which can predispose a child to many forms of anti-social behavior. This consequent anti-social behavior may range from stealing, firesetting, running away, sexual promiscuity, to other forms of juvenile delinquency or, in some youngsters, to suicide. (Dizmang 1970, p. 33).

Of the many feeling states associated with suicidal behavior, the most characteristic are feelings of human isolation and withdrawal. Conflicting home situations compound a youth's sense of isolation until it becomes intolerable.

From our sample we singled out 458 youths from the most troubled home situations. Nearly three in five (57%) of these youth say they sometimes consider suicide. (This is similar to the 62% of low self-esteem youth who admitted the same.) Conflict in one's home does indeed precipitate thoughts of death.

Differences between youth from troubled homes, and all other youth, are illustrated in table 7. We singled out those youth who scored in the top quartile of the scales, Concern over Family Unity and Parental Pressures.

TABLE 7

Percentage of Youth Much Bothered by Thoughts of Death

Item	Percentage Much Bothered	
	Youth from Troubled Homes N = 458	All Other Youth N = 6592
I sometimes think of dying or being killed.	48	27
I get into moods where I can't seem to cheer up.	63	35
Life is such a mess—sometimes I wish I could "get away from it all."	72	42

One should be concerned when an adolescent becomes withdrawn, careless of his appearance, unable to concentrate, disinterested in academic work, and shows apathy and fatigue. These are some of the commonly observed symptoms of the depression that precedes suicide.

Lest the correlation between family ill health and low self-esteem be overempahsized, it should be noted that a large minority of youth whose families are in turmoil do not entertain thoughts of suicide. Many cope with their situations and rise above the stress. Where this is true, however, a history of stable home life probably preceded the stress.

A study of 8,865 high-school youth in Toronto portrays the link between youth and parental behavior. These data collected in 1970 on drug usage established a positive link between parental drug use and the frequency and amount of drug use by children. The study contradicts the long held belief that "turning on" with drugs is due only to a generation gap of youthful defiance.

The percentage of students who reported using tobacco, marijuana, barbiturates, heroin, speed, LSD, and other mind-affecting drugs was lowest if the parents used neither tobacco nor alcohol. Mothers who smoked and drank frequently were most likely to have their children turn to illicit and stronger drugs, the study indicated.

Students who reported their parents to be regular users of tranquilizers (the survey was confidential) were twice as likely to smoke marijuana, three times as likely to use hallucinatory drugs, and eight times as likely to follow the example of drug use set in their households.

Such information illustrates why youth cannot be understood except in the social context of their environment and especially their family. Working with the adolescent must involve working with the parents as well. The full development of young people may require changed parents.

Toward Family Health

Changing parental attitudes is an appropriate goal for religious institutions, whose business is to change beliefs and values. Fortunately, we know of ways to accomplish such changes. As parents are helped to love each other, to establish a climate of trust, and to begin communicating with their teenage children a revolution ensues in the home. At least half the parents of church youth would profit from education to bring about such changes.

Our basic task is not to solve people's problems, but to provide what is needed so that they can assume responsibility for their own situations. We can provide a point of view, viable options, a supportive environment, and a way to respond selectively to available options.

A Point of View

When we view the heartache one person brings on another, we discern the pervasive quality of man's sinfulness. It stimulates one's appetite to control, manipulate, and dominate people. Its fruit is a hardness of heart that is especially devastating in the close confines of a family.

Paradoxically, though one's family shapes (some people would say "determines") his behavior, God holds every person responsible for his actions. Scripture makes this abundantly clear and for good reason. All of us, parents and youth alike, are adept at buck-passing; it began with Adam blaming Eve. We prefer to blame our wrongdoings on the failures and sins of others and in so doing run away from responsibility.

One who relates to troubled youth should be clear on this: each person is responsible for his actions. No one should be allowed to excuse his irresponsibility on the grounds that it was caused by others' treatment of him.

Each person in a troubled home has the possibility of changing his response to the situation. Though powerfully influenced, he is still free to act. How a young person has been treated limits his options, but does not determine his response. Though determinism is the basic fabric of the physical universe, choice within a limited framework is the fact of human existence.

Viable Options

Our task is to make hope-inspiring contacts with troubled youth and parents, to make them aware of their options, and then to help them make a choice and commitment. By responding selectively, each person can allow into his life what he knows will change him.

One dynamic force that is seldom understood is the life-changing awareness of God's forgiveness. This is one of the possibilities that troubled families need to discover.

Another option focuses upon some kind of educational experience which translates large theological concepts into everyday language and application. One such educational program, called Parent/Adult Covenant Theatre,[4] uses two weekend retreats to train parents in reflection, active listening, responding to a child, facing his own problems, and resolving conflicts. Another is Parent Effectiveness Training developed by Thomas Gordon.[5] Convinced that most parents sincerely want to raise emotionally healthy children but lack the insight and skills to do so, Gordon has developed a systematic program of training for the job of parenthood. It has proved effective in modifying parent-child relationships; parents often need not therapy but education about human relationships.

Support Group

In his book *A Nation of Strangers* (1972) Vance Packard draws an upsetting picture of Americans as an increasingly isolated society without roots and without the capacity to enter into deep, lasting relationships. His description also applies to youth and parents, many of whom belong to a "family of strangers." They need a group that gives them the feeling of being uniquely valued and the support that is unavailable in their own families.

Adults who work with youth in a church setting must give increasing emphasis to the "nonkindred family" made up of friends. Young people who do not have a kindred family need a church fellowship which provides the experience of communicating in depth and the security of people with whom they can identify. The church of Jesus Christ has a history, a tradition, a people, and a style of life that can become the only "family" some youth will experience.

That a family approach can make a unique contribution to a program of Christian education is being recognized and applied in many places. Note what one of my reviewers penned on the side of her manuscript: "We have started a family Sunday school class at home with three families because our children object to the 'school' approach on Sunday morning. We have a class of eighteen ranging in age from four to forty-five."

The benefits of "nonkindred families" are real and measurable. In a large research study called Youth Reaching Youth[6] we found that group-oriented programs which taught friendship skills also developed support groups which served as "family" experiences. At the end of seventeen months of weekly meetings (with appropriate control groups) the following changes were recorded:

1. Self-esteem increased dramatically, and self-criticism and personal anxiety decreased.
2. The youth increased measurably in their openness to people and ideas; they learned to share themselves with parents and to be more self-disclosing with their clergymen.[7]

I can sit down and think about the world
and the war, and I just cry.

An eighteen-year-old girl

4   Cry of Social Protest

Jeannie is intelligent, pretty, always busy in the way that bright
high-school students tend to be, sparkling with enthusiasm, full of
giggles and life at parties—a thoroughly charming girl. She is a
leader in both her high school and her church youth group. Her
college education is being financed by a fund her parents started
before she was born. You would never guess that she has anything
to be troubled about.

During her high-school career, she cried out for help in a way
no one noticed. She came into a meeting of youth-group officers
one evening looking very thoughtful. That morning she had gone
with a group from her high school to visit a home for the mentally
retarded. She was silent during the early part of the meeting; then
all at once, apropos of nothing, she said grimly, "I get so darned
disgusted, sometimes, when we sit here and haggle about whether
we want to invite the ninth graders in on our next party, and what
we're going to do at the party, and all that kind of junk, when
there are people living in old people's homes, and hospitals, and
places for mentally retarded people who don't have anybody to
care about them. And people are starving, and people are fighting
. . ." She broke off, conscious that others were staring. "I just wish
sometimes we did something that really mattered, that made a
difference to people who need so much and who don't . . ." she
trailed off, lamely. After a pause the meeting got back on the rails
and settled the necessary details for the party.

The voice of social conscience is not always loud and insistent. It will not always come on strong, like the boisterous brashness of one covering up his feelings of worthlessness, or the stormy tears of the girl who longs for peace in her home. The signals of social concern that high-school students send require a special alertness. They may come subtly, infrequently, or perhaps in such an exaggerated form that the impulse is to laugh and forget them, or, perhaps, to refuse to allow them to be put into action through the church.

The concern may surface as a quiet question asked in private, following a sermon or program meant to stir the social conscience. It may show itself in a boy's withdrawing from the youth group and getting to work on a political campaign. It may be a request to talk privately or in group discussions about social issues—war, poverty, discrimination.

Our studies show that many of the socially concerned are solid humanists who do not believe in the gospel; as bright, well-adjusted, and sensitive people, these change-oriented youth are some of the "unbelieving" critics of the church. An equal proportion of the youth described in this chapter, however, reflect a knowledge of the Christian faith and a love for their church.

Youth of both motivations are sufficiently bright, sophisticated, and mature to have grasped the message of the gospel and to hold it up against their church's track record on social action. Their expressions of that comparison may sound harsh, critical, and hard to take, but they are another way of sounding the cry.

The sensitive youth worker or parent will be alert to indications of concern. More than that, recognizing that the concern is often there but unexpressed, he will provide opportunities for expression. It is the clear message of our data that the concerns are there.

This chapter focuses on youth whose cries of anger over injustice became a cacophony during the years 1965–70. They can be distinguished by means of five major characteristics. They are: (1) humanitarian, (2) oriented to change, (3) socially involved, (4) concerned over national issues, and (5) critical of the institutional church, in which adults seem not to be "caring."

In 1969, a cry of protest erupted on college campuses throughout the United States as students demanded an end to the war in Vietnam. By the spring of 1970 a majority of college students were opposed to fighting in any form whether for the purpose of containing Communists, maintaining a position of power in the world, or upholding our honor as a first-rate power. For them the compelling cause in life was social justice. Wrongs being done to people had to be righted, and these students were of a mind to bring about needed changes without further delays.

Though a majority of the college youth rejected the philosophy of violence, many employed acts of violence as the only means strong enough to gain their ends. Most students resisted the tactics of radical activists, but sympathized with their goals. High-school students, too, were antiwar and concerned over what was happening in their world. A large percentage were sympathetic to the protest movement and many joined the parades and mass demonstrations.

During this historic period, leaders of time-honored institutions like churches and schools cast worried glances toward the future. In discussion I found a group of leading Minneapolis businessmen preoccupied with student attacks on big business and fearful that student reaction would roll like a tidal wave into their future and adversely affect the economy of the country.

Our research team, interviewing college and seminary presidents, denominational administrators, and church educators and leaders in preparation for Youth Research Center's *A Study of Generations*, met these same fears for the future. Will today's youth remain within the institutional church? Will they, as tomorrow's leaders, support established congregations? Nothing was voiced oftener in the interviews than concern over what was happening among students and youth.

Meanwhile, mass media, assuming this to be their legitimate news function, played up the violence, destruction of property, and confrontations. The inevitable result was a general loss of perspective. Many students joined causes they did not understand, taking part as if protests were a new form of fun and games. Their antics, usually featured by the media, infuriated segments of the public. Sharp polarization began to be apparent.

By the spring of 1970, student provocations which had dominated the news for many months had awakened a slumbering grizzly bear of public reaction. Understanding and sympathy for student causes shifted to anger and resentment. Adults who had looked indulgently at the antics of young idealists of the "now generation" began to refer to "troublemakers and spoiled brats." A crescendo of angry voices demanded cutbacks in student subsidies and an end to one-sided demands and simplistic prescriptions for instant change.

The high watermark in youth's unrest and rebellion came at Kent State University on May 4, 1970, when an order to fire on antiwar demonstrators left four young people dead and nine wounded.

This tragedy and its aftermath brought to a point of high visibility the polarization of opinion and feeling that had been gathering through the spring. Many of the older generation approved the order to fire as a necessary step toward restoring law and order, deplorable though the consequences were. Dramatizing this same belief that authority *must* be asserted and order restored, on May 8, 1970, a group of construction workers on New York's Wall Street disrupted a parade of antiwar demonstrators and manhandled some of the young demonstrators.

Students, on the other hand, reacted to the Kent State "massacre" with horror and anger. On May 10, 448 universities and colleges were either closed or on strike. The spirit of protest also involved many high schools, some of which experienced protest walkouts and teach-ins with many students participating.

May, 1970, a high point in the radical political action which had been mounting through the '60s, was the time during which our survey was taken.

One can expect that our survey data would reflect youth's feelings about social injustice. A cry of anger, disappointment, and sometimes outrage has been and always will be heard within the church. It is the cry of the peacemakers, the merciful, the friends of outcasts. It comes from those who are pained by the sufferings of others and unable to tolerate a *status quo* that does little to alter the lot of needy people. The distinctive characteristics of the socially concerned youth are shown in figure 4.

We singled out 335 socially concerned youth with characteristics like those shown in the figure 4.[1] Then we compared them with all others, using 420 items from the survey to determine where they resemble all other church youth and where they are distinctly different.

In general, they identify, more than other church youth, with the sufferings of people. They are inwardly pained when they see minorities abused, they worry about world starvation, and are troubled when they see people in need. They want to become involved in effecting changes that will push the realities of life closer to the oft-repeated ideals of church and government.

Socially concerned youth tend to be bright, with many more drawing above average grades than typifies church youth in general. More of them have parents who are in a profession or have a college or graduate school background.

They say they take time to think through why they believe and act as they do, and more say their beliefs and values have changed in the past year or so. What these changes are cannot be learned from this survey, but they appear to be in values and in their concept of what is important in life. In doctrinal beliefs, religious practices, and involvement in the life of the congregation socially concerned youth answer as do all church youth.

In ranking a variety of life values, more of the socially concerned list money as of "least importance"; physical appearance or attractiveness gets a low billing for nearly half these youth. A large number credit meaningful work with "extreme importance," and the majority insist that a person should look out not only for himself but also for the welfare of others. These values and beliefs are associated with their heightened sensitivity to the needs of others. One illustration is in the area of race relations. Many more of this socially concerned group than usual see themselves as more liberal in their opinions than their parents.

**characteristics of
socially
concerned
youth**

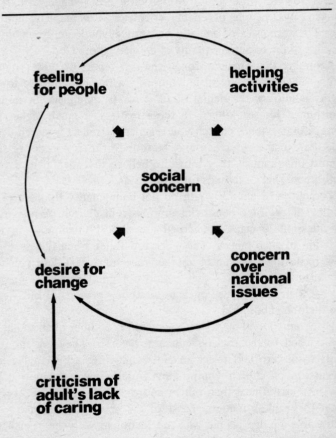

feeling
for people

helping
activities

social
concern

desire for
change

concern
over
national
issues

criticism of
adult's lack
of caring

Heaviness of arrow indicates strength of intercorrelation.

Feeling for People

As indicated by figure 4, a strong characteristic of socially concerned and involved youth is their humanitarian attitude and feeling for people who are commonly condemned. This attitude reflects the presence of an openmindedness, sensitivity, and compassion toward those who are often criticized and judged harshly; blacks, Jews, people of enemy countries, Communists, and the like. The responses of socially concerned youth imply an understanding of the essential equality of all men before God.

A quality that shines through the self-report of these youth is mercy. They reject almost unanimously a punitive attitude toward enemy countries, the denial of food for Communists, or unusual punishment for sex killers. In these matters, a much higher percentage than typifies church youth generally reflect a merciful attitude. Part of the difference may be found in their concept of God. Almost unanimously they refuse to believe that mental illness is a punishment that God sends for certain sins.

Though most church youth do not countenance the idea of excluding blacks or other racial groups from church or nonchurch activities, the socially concerned are almost unanimous in their rejection of such tactics. Though a few falter when the issue narrows to having a person of another race for a next-door neighbor, the large majority agree they would not mind. Again, a majority believe their families are open to accepting persons of other races into their neighborhood.

Discernment and clarity of conviction is another quality that can be attached to the socially concerned youth. They are far more likely to discern and reject an anti-Semitic remark than the large population of church youth; they largely reject the notion that Jews are less ethical than others and that Jews are more likely to cheat in business matters. Most of the socially concerned youth refuse to prejudge people who are identified with the Jewish race or faith.

Openness to people is associated with an openness to the findings of science. Most socially concerned youth do not believe that science and Christianity fight each other and therefore reject the idea of their incompatibility.

The evidence seems clear. One finds within the church extremely perceptive and sensitive youth who cry out in protest over the way some people are being treated. They associate their convictions with Christianity, being convinced that the elimination of all racial discrimination is a goal of Christianity. Their sensitivities also deter them from agreeing with commonly heard criticism of the poor; they resist the assertion that most poor people could alter their lot if they only took advantage of their opportunities.

Desire for Change

To some people, a liberal is a bad guy, a conservative, the good guy. Those who think this way always have difficulty with the person of Christ who in many ways was a liberal and a revolutionary and whose disciples were said to be "turning the world upside down."

Socially concerned youth are more liberal in their approach to life and more ready to break with traditions. This may mean radical changes or a nostalgic return to the past. Perhaps you, too, know young people who have said: "I plan to adopt children of different colors and nationalities so that my children . . . will think in terms of the individual rather than the color of his skin or where he was born" (Sabine 1971, p. 22).

"Who wants to live in a world of concrete and paved roads? We should melt down every automobile, destroy all highways and paved roads, take down all skyscrapers, and return to dirt roads and use horses" (Sabine 1971, p. 111).

From our data, however, we can learn what changes they especially want. Among 200 possibilities, we find that six items draw a heightened response from the socially concerned: the war, military service, the unlikelihood of peace, an unresponsive government, social injustice, and the chasm between professed ideals and the realities of everyday life.

The shock that these youth feel as they reach their teen years is described in this young person's statement:

In the American education system, each child receives the impression that America is a great, strong, nearly infallible country. America is the magic land of opportunity where Cinderellas and Horatio Algers run rampant, where God is always on our side, where every wrong is righted with blind yet merciful justice. What a shock it is for the child later to realize that America does have corrupt legislators, unfair laws, apathetic citizens. How horrible to discover that America was not always on "the right side" in foreign affairs in the past and is not now; to see that its foreign aid policies and programs are motivated at least as much by ultimate financial and political gains as by altruism (Sabine 1971, p. 120).

Because the tragedy of war troubles these youth most, one can expect opposition to military conscription. Most assert that war is basically wrong and that a citizen should have the right to decide in which wars he will fight. Here they part company with a large segment of other church youth.

The same concern appears in their rejection of this statement: "Every young man should be willing to serve in the armed forces." One young person put it this way:

All through our lives in school, we have been taught the meaning of freedom, etc. But when it comes to wanting our rights and freedoms as human beings and free people, the so-called democratic society tells us we have no freedoms or rights. They say we are immature and not responsible enough. Yet we are given a number, a gun, and the right to kill (Sabine 1971, p. 123).

The personal tragedy with which many teenagers feel they live is expressed by another young person:

When you see one of your close friends leave for Vietnam, you know you'll never know him again. Even if he comes back, what he has lived in over there has affected his mind and changed him completely (Sabine 1971, pp. 116–17).

Church leaders can expect that youth who feel the urgency of world tragedy will ask their church to take a stand on some of the issues. These youth believe that churches and synagogues should be more involved in social, political, and economic issues. They also believe that students should have more to say about what is taught in high school. If they believe their input has merit for the school, it is reasonable to assume they feel the same about the church on matters related to social action. If given a chance, they will probably speak.

As would be expected, the socially concerned are generally ready to support legislation that provides free medical care and adequate housing for everyone, irrespective of their ability to pay.

Another example of their people-oriented stance is their quite unanimous rejection of the statement, "It is wrong to date a person of another race." They also disagree that people of any color have the right to keep others out of their neighborhood. Here the socially concerned have strong support from all other church youth because three-fourths of them join in disagreeing with that statement.

In the area of sexual ethics we become aware of two life-styles among socially concerned youth. About half of them believe that "as long as you love the other person, sexual intercourse before marriage is okay." Less than a third of other church youth feel that way.

Further evidence in contrasting life-styles is seen in drug usage. Of the socially concerned, two out of five fight inner battles over the rightness of taking drugs (pot, LSD, or mind-changing drugs) compared with one-fourth of other church youth. Among the socially concerned 26% have been or are now using drugs, contrasted with 14% of other church youth. Similarly, more of the socially concerned sometimes get high on alcohol (45% versus 30%).

The mingling of these two life-styles among the socially concerned has hindered some people from accepting their protest. Some adults justify their *status quo* position by associating social reforms solely with "long-hair drug addicts." The association is neither valid nor true to the facts; our studies find two distinct groups of people calling for greater involvement in social issues. One speaks out of a sense of mission, love, and conscience. In this group, the social conscience of some is rooted in Christian commitment and of others in a non-Christian humanism. The second group, though using a similar rhetoric, reflects a different orientation. Here one finds both advocates and enemies of social action—youth who see the conflict as a power struggle. Herein are seeds of the tyranny and bigotry of both right and left (Strommen et al. 1972, p. 290).

Our data on church youth show that a minority of the socially concerned youth speak out of a life orientation of pessimism, distrust, and general anger with life that characterizes some in the second group. To become involved in a power struggle appears to be more than their way of acknowledging the underdog. It is also a way to gain attention and significance for themselves while displaying some of their anger against authority.

Helping Activities

A sign of growing maturity is the ability to feel for individuals other than oneself, for groups other than one's own. Socially involved youth show this maturity of spirit in their sensitivity to abused minorities. They suffer over the thought of starving people and are distressed when they observe their peers headed for tragedy. Less troubling is the knowledge that someone else does not have a personal faith although only a fourth of our sample show no concern over their friends' lack of faith.

There are many ways of expressing concern for others and varying motivations for being helpful. In this study, social action is positively linked to social concern and religious commitment. Some are driven to action by sensitivity to world problems; others, by gratitude for a personal faith. Both motivations characterize the majority of socially concerned youth.

The question is often raised about socially concerned youth: Are they actually doing anything to help others, or do they only criticize society? Our data is heartening; it reveals that a majority of these youth are involved in these ways:

1. I have tried to be a friend to people who are lonely or rejected.
2. In my home I have raised questions about issues of social concern.
3. I have spoken up to defend persons or minority groups who are being ridiculed.

4. I have been involved in discussions on how the Christian should relate to issues of social concern (for example, civil rights, the aging, student protest, war).
5. I have spent time in a program of service to others.
6. I give some of my money for people in need.
7. In the past month I have told someone what my faith means to me.
8. In the past few months I have tried to help someone who needed personal assistance (for example, free babysitting, yard work, help to an ill or handicapped person).

Concern over National Issues

In April, 1971, a representative group of 920 American youth assembled at Estes Park, Colorado, for a White House Conference on Youth. Distressed over the chasm between the ideals of the Constitution and the realities of life, they drew up an eloquent message of concern. The preamble to their list of 550 recommendations and resolutions on social issues began with these words:

> We are in the midst of a political, social, and cultural revolution. Uncontrolled technology and the exploitation of people by people threaten to dehumanize our society. We must affirm the recognition of Life as the Supreme Value which will not bear manipulation for other ends.

Feelings about a worsening future are strong in concerned church youth; they are much bothered by the specter of human life being destroyed by pollution. Well over half are likewise troubled by the violence and mayhem on city streets. The future appears to them to promise more violence, revolution, and eventually total destruction of this country. Though the word *Armageddon* is not familiar, it stands as a frightening prospect for many.

Ranking next to this overwhelming fear of the future is a frustration with the government. Youth are much troubled by the apparent unresponsiveness of the president and legislative bodies to the needs of people. About a third of them are equally bothered by those citizens who give up on their government and seek only to destroy it.

On the average, four out of five church youth express some degree of concern over all eleven of the national issues listed. Though it is a small group that cries out in protest, a majority of church youth are concerned over the national situation. This comment typifies their attitude:

> Our parents and teachers have tried to bring us up thinking that America is almost perfect and infallible—and we wish it were. Unfortunately, we've found that our nation and our society have many faults, and we wish to attempt to remedy these ailments.

Criticism of Adult Caring

Youth most distressed over social ills also express the greatest disappointment in their church. As social consciousness heightens, criticism of the church mounts.

Such criticism was widespread at the time this survey was made. The task force on religion at the White House Conference on Youth summarized the conviction of the 920 representative leadership youth by saying:

> We believe that youth seeks the following values in religion but too often finds them lacking in our religious institutions and teachings:
>
> Leadership and guidance in coping with the problems youth face, such as the draft, drugs, destruction of the environment, racism, and loss of identity.
>
> Relevance of religious teachings to the problems of present-day society.
>
> Realism in religious teachings, so as to provide teachings freed of meaningless dogma and credible for the individual in the modern world.
>
> An influence that brings men together instead of separating them; fosters unity and brotherhood instead of division and prejudice.
>
> Action that really offers solutions to our national problems and a clear sense of national priorities, instead of adherence to outworn parochialism.

We believe that failures and negative influences traceable to religion stem not from the religious values themselves but from failures to put these teachings into practice, and from the hypocrisy that would use them to justify self-interest and prejudice (Greene 1971).

Similarly, youth of this chapter voice criticisms of their church but not the facile criticisms of intellectual roughnecks who rush onto the national scene like gangbusters. Most of the socially concerned young people described in this chapter have deep attachments to their congregations and reflect attitudes similar to other church youth. It is at church that they meet their best friends and see adults whom they know. Four out of five are likely to hear their names called out by some adult when attending a service. Most of them acknowledge the kindness of many adults and appreciate that they are quick to help the sick or needy. They agree, too, that church teaching has much to say about life as it really is. Yet they are disappointed in their church.

About half feel that adults: (1) seriously consider doing something about current social problems; (2) are concerned about world starvation, war, poverty; (3) seek ways to respond more meaningfully to human needs; (4) are interested in the youth; (5) make young people feel welcome at a service. The other half do not agree or are not sure where the adults stand.

The critique gains a majority when it focuses on what the congregation fails to do as a corporate group; socially concerned youth would not want to "follow the example of my congregation in its stand on social problems." They are convinced that most adults in their congregation would not "be able to tell you what the purpose of our church is."

The unpleasant fact is that many socially concerned youth do not believe their church will accept a family of another race into their community, nor will they welcome people who look different (richer, poorer, another race, different in hair or dress). Many do not think their church is doing anything about problems of social concern (e.g., housing, racism, injustice, civil rights) or trying to improve parent-youth relationships. Though they see individual concern, they feel it is not expressed *organizationally* by the congregation.

Example is a powerful educational tool, both for negative as well as positive teaching. Most youth, though aware of the goodwill and sincerity of individual members, look with dismay at the little their congregations are doing. They may prejudge the church as adults are prone to prejudge youth. Sometimes, of course, their dismay is due to lack of *knowing* what is being done.

But their critique cannot be dismissed as mere reflections of unhappy people; if negativism were involved it would show in other ways as well. Neither can it be dismissed as the voice of outsiders. These young people are both altruistic and solid members of their congregations. The cause of offense is more likely the unresponsiveness of congregations to deep and immediate needs or, perhaps, to youth's ignorance of what is actually being done.

It has not been the habit of adults to listen seriously to youth. Listening comes hardest when youth are critical of adult action, particularly when adults already feel guilt about their inaction. Yet that painful listening must be done.

Proportion of Socially Concerned

It is difficult to estimate the percentage of church youth who are socially concerned; a precise answer requires that we use as criteria all the characteristics given in this chapter. When the ecumenical sample is divided using the three strongest predictors of a humanitarian attitude, we have the following rough estimate:

54%—Think about why they believe and act as they do. (They score above average in humanitarian attitudes.)

32%—Do as indicated above *and* achieve excellent or above average grades. (They score higher on humanitarian attitudes.)

9%—Do as indicated on the above criteria *and* are strongly oriented to change. (They score the highest on humanitarian attitudes.)

On this basis, one can conclude that one in ten is a militant for change.

Surrounding them is a larger group which, though less eager for change, is sensitive to and concerned about social injustice. Combined, the groups account for one-third of church youth.

Responding to the Cry

Listening to the cry of these youth is like listening to the voice of conscience. Who can fault them as they ask their churches to become more involved in social ministries? They see clearly the danger of the church losing its real mission, as expressed by Dr. James Shannon.

> The church that is firmly established in members, in money, and in status is a prime candidate for the "establishment" club. It finds it all too easy to link arms and identify with all the other establishments of this world than to keep its pristine sensitivity for the poor, the sick, the blind and the disenfranchised who have no power, no voice and no prestige save their badges of need, poverty, illness and loneliness (*Minneapolis Sunday Tribune*, 12 November 1972).

A fitting response to the cry is to establish forms of congregational life that express what is latent within a majority of adults. A congregation needs to say clearly, "We care," and to say it with a language of action.

More immediate steps are suggested by the kinds of help opportunities the young people prefer. From descriptions of forty programs and activities that could be available in their churches, they declared their specific preferences and said, "I am very much interested and would go out of my way to participate."

Most attractive is belonging to a group where there is candor and caring among the members. Four out of five would go out of their way to attend meetings where people "felt free to say what they really think" and to experience acceptance among people "who really care about each other."

Three out of four express preference for a project that involves serving people in their community; they want training in being a friend to the lonely and rejected, insight into making changes in their schools, and growth in their concern and love for others. Truly, there are youth in congregations who are willing to match rhetoric with action.

Another interest relates to clarifying beliefs and values. Three out of four want to find meaning and purpose to life; they want exposure to people of other religious beliefs and chances to discuss their doubts and conflicts openly; they want to overcome their lack of self-confidence.

Attractive also are meetings with adults to discuss problems such as military service, participation in recreational activities, experiences which teach how to be mature with others, discussions of a Christian perspective on war, activities where one learns how to speak about one's faith, interchanges which increase self-understanding, and opportunities to receive the friendship and encouragement of loyal adults.

The eagerness of these youth to learn from adults is self-evident. Though oriented to change, they do not fit the newspaper stereotypes of youth who damn the establishment and listen only to their own age group.

Youth Reaching Youth

One of youth's concerns is their own age group. They worry about some of their contemporaries and wish they could reach out to them in a helping way. Given training, they can become an important resource for contacting lonely and alienated youth.

In 1970, the Youth Research Center launched a three-year test of the relative effectiveness of three programs which train high-school youth to reach out to the friendless. The project, funded by the National Institute of Mental Health, involved 276 high-school juniors who met weekly for seventeen months of training and outreach. During this time they established friendships with 493 persons, some of whom were like the girl described by one of the Junior Volunteers.

> She was teased unmercifully by so many, many kids—on the bus home, in school. She seemed so alone, and she didn't know how to to keep kids from teasing her. She egged them on by her reactions; so many kids would come right out and be mean to her. I guess it looked like she needed to know there was someone who wouldn't always hound her.

A real and meaningful friendship was formed by the Junior Volunteer which lasted through most of the girl's senior year. Some indication of how this girl and the other 492 "reached" youth felt about the relationship appears in the following transcript of an interview.

Reached: I've known her (Project Youth Volunteer) for about two years, but our friendship really started developing around the fall of this year. I came to her with a problem that I had gotten myself into trouble with, and she helped me. I had lost a few friends, and I was pretty much alone, by myself. And I didn't have my closest friend; we had sort of grown away from each other.

Interviewer: You have known her for approximately how many months?

Reached: Closely I've known her for about seven months. We're together in school every day, and we'll see each other off and on when we don't have classes.

She takes time to listen to me; she'll sit down if I have a problem, and she'll talk it out with me. Or if she notices that I'm doing something weird that she doesn't like in me and she doesn't think that it's good for me to do, she'll sit down and talk to me about it. She'll tell me; she'll just say what she feels. It's really nice to have somebody that will help you around. She'll listen to people; she'll listen to their problems. And, she's an outgoing person; I really like her.

Interviewer: Any other points that you really like about her?

Reached: She's fun to be with. She and I have some common ideas and similar problems. We sort of came together. . . .

Reached: I really like having a close friend, someone I can call up and say, "Hey, do you want to do something tonight?" Go over to her house or she'll come over to mine. Like my parents are going out for the week-

> end and she's coming over and staying with me; and
> go boating and sailing, all kinds of things. It's really
> good to have a close friend.

Observable changes in the behavior of the "reached" youth—
some more than would be expected, a few well beyond expectation
—were recorded.

They are listed in table 8 with an indication of *how many* were
reported by sixty-three "reached" youth who were interviewed.
Scores ranging from −2 to +2 indicate degree of positive or negative change. A score of +1 represents behavioral change that is
better than would be expected. A score of 2 represents the best
that could happen—as perceived by the reacher.

TABLE 8
Changes in the Behavior of "Reached" Youth

No. of Reached Youth	Dimension of Growth	Degree of Change
3	Consideration for others	+ 1.67
7	Ability to establish and carry out goals regarding education	+ 1.29
4	Reduction in drug use	+ 1.25
16	Ability to confide in others	+ .94
7	Ability to cope with school responsibilities	+ .71
6	Ability to communicate with the opposite sex	+ .71
16	Sense of worth and confidence	+ .69
3	Church participation and strengthening of faith	+ .67
20	Ability to make and keep friends	+ .65
13	Ability to communicate with parents	+ .42
6	Trusting and accepting of others	+ .42
7	Ability to face problems, accept criticism, and make decisions	+ .36

The purpose of this government-funded project was to assess the
likelihood of training core-youth in religious institutions to offer
friendship to friendless youth. Not only was this purpose achieved,
but the 274 reachers themselves benefited in observable ways:

increase in self-regard, greater willingness to participate in self-disclosure with persons not too distant from them, less worried about being accepted by others, and increased self-confidence. Socially concerned youth profit from training opportunities and prove effective in reaching lonely peers.

We want God's commandments to
be followed, not preached out both
sides of mouths.

Sabine

5   Cry of the Prejudiced

Psychologist James Dittes, writing about prejudice and religion in
Research on Religious Development (1971) makes this important
point. The Scriptures cite two type of "believers"—those for whom
religion is a thoughtful commitment affecting the total person, and
those for whom religion is a formal and externalized response. Old
Testament prophets distinguished between solemn assemblies that
were a mockery and a righteousness which is like an overflowing
stream, between burnt offerings that are a duty and a knowledge of
God which is coupled with a steadfast love.

Christ underscored the distinction between public, overt, institu-
tionalized, self-serving religion and an inner response of contrition,
trust, commitment, and dedication. He made uncompromising attacks on the pious Pharisees, saying, "They do all their deeds to be
seen by men." In addressing the Pharisees he said, "You tithe . . .
but neglect the weightier matters of . . . mercy. . . . You are sons
of those who murdered the prophets."

He clearly denounced men who use religion for personal gain,
who are willing to destroy whoever threatens them or their establishment.

Since the days of Christ and the prophets, people have made
similar observations about the religion of man. Kierkegaard distinguished between "official Christianity" and the "radical Christian." Barth and others made distinctions between Christianity and
religion. Let us illustrate in terms of a fictional young person.

One thing you can say for Chuck—when his youth group is meeting, he is usually there. He prides himself on seldom missing a meeting, as though he has earned something to which more casual members of the group are not entitled.

Chuck is selfish about his group. His slowness to accept new members sometimes irritates others, and several members were embarrassed by his behavior when one member brought a foreign exchange student from Africa to a meeting. It takes new people a long time to gain Chuck's respect and confidence.

He tends not to be very accepting of people who haven't made up their minds about discussion issues or who disagree with him. His "convictions" are stereotyped prejudgments that he accepts, in closed-mind fashion, and champions. He knows where he stands on legalization of marijuana, abortion, current political issues, questions of dating behavior, and the rehabilitation of those who break the law. Once he has expressed his opinion, no matter what else turns up during the discussion, Chuck rarely changes his mind.

Worship appears to be important to him, but he is less enthusiastic about participating in an improvised worship service during a contemporary celebration of worship on a weekend retreat. It does not seem to him that he has really gone to church.

Though fairly well accepted by most of his group, he is roundly opposed when he sounds off on social issues.

Social scientists have found prejudice in people who adhere to social forms of religion and not in those who "take religion seriously in a more internalized sense." Adorno (1950) noted that prejudiced people "seem to make use of religious ideas in order to gain some immediate practical advantage or aid in the manipulation of people."

Gordon Allport, noting this utilitarianism, distinguished between "intrinsic" and "extrinsic" religious persons. Extrinsically religious persons use their religion, and the intrinsically religious live theirs, says Allport. The extrinsic personality institutionalizes religion; the intrinsic person wants an "interiorized" faith.

This distinction provides understanding of youth like Chuck: the sometimes pious but prejudiced. Their profiles express an attitude which unfortunately appears within the Christian church at large. It is the cry of Archie Bunkers, racists, and bigots, who pride themselves on being self-made men. "Don't disturb our little world," they say. "Don't let outsiders in." It is the cry of people whose religion is self-effort and whose goal is achieving a place in the sun, even at the price of stepping on others. Although it is more common among people in advanced in years, our findings indicate that this outlook is alive and active in the youth population as well.

Allen and Spilka, building on the early studies already mentioned, offer a distinction between "committed religious" and "consensual religious." Briefly, the criteria groups were these.[1]

> The "committed religious" conceptualize their faith in relational expressions; they speak of their faith with clarity, make distinctions that show an awareness of complex issues, are thoughtful about their beliefs, open to new insights, and show that their faith is a personal concern and of central importance. They seek to make it relevant to daily activities.
>
> The "consensual religious" conceptualize their faith in specific dos and don'ts, they speak of it in vague and conventional statements, they oversimplify the issues, resist differing ideas and insist always that theirs are the right beliefs. The consensual rarely apply their faith in daily activities and behavior.

Allen and Spilka found that two out of three "consensual" respondents were prejudiced but no more than one out of ten of the "committed."

These two orientations are parallel to the law orientation and gospel orientation of *A Study of Generations*. In this chapter we will adopt the consensual-committed distinction.

It should be understood that some youth fall between the two orientations by combining both emphases to a relatively equal degree. And some espouse and manifest *neither* by any great degree.

Do-It-Yourself Religion

More than youth of the other four groups, the consensual religionist holds to a generalized religion that stresses man's efforts to achieve the favor of God. Their quite consistent theological stance is noteworthy because consistency of response to doctrinal items is not a characteristic of church youth generally. Even committed

youth who embrace the Christian faith with enthusiasm and participate actively in their congregations have not learned to make the
theological distinction.

The following data show how many youth consistently accept or
reject items associated with achieving God's favor.

> 83%—The way to be accepted by God is to try sincerely to live a
> good life. (Yes or Not Sure)

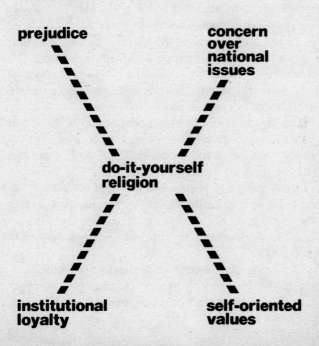

**characteristics of
prejudiced
youth**

prejudice

concern
over
national
issues

do-it-yourself
religion

institutional
loyalty

self-oriented
values

75%—The above statement *and* "God is satisfied if a person lives
the best life he can." (Yes or Not Sure)

49%—The two above statements *and* "If I say I believe in God and
do right I will get to heaven." (Yes or Not Sure)

42%—The three above statements *and* "I believe a person at birth
is neither good nor bad." (Yes or Not Sure)

32%—All of the above statements with an exclusive "Yes" to the
first item.

If church youth in general have not formulated a consistent
theology, how do youth labeled "consensual" differ in what they
believe? A sample was drawn of 538 youth who most resemble the
characteristics of the chart (figure 5). (They score in the lower
quarter on Biblical Concepts, lower half on Human Relations, and
the upper half on Adult Caring.) A profile emerges when we compare these 538 youth with the other 6,512.

Consensual youth exhibit greater consistency in affirming that
salvation is gained by earning God's pleasure. Almost unanimously
they agree that "to try sincerely to live a good life" is the way to be
accepted by God. It matters little to them what one believes as
long as he is sincere and lives the best life he can. The gospel for
these youth is essentially composed of God's rules for right living.
Whoever follows God's rule book—the Bible—and plays the game
right will make it. Everyone can win if he chooses to because he is
born neither good or bad. Outside intervention does not appear to
be an essential ingredient in man's relationship to God. Christianity is viewed simplistically as something man does (see table 9).

The you-can-do-it-if-you-try conviction described here seems to
color the attitudes of these youth toward the less fortunate. Two-
thirds believe that most people who live in poverty could do something about it if they really wanted to. Seventy-two percent agree
that poor people do not take advantage of opportunities available
to them. The work ethic is tied up with their achievement concept
of Christianity.

The dominant and distinguishing feature of consensual youth
appears to be greater consistency in affirming a religion that
stresses achievement, right living, and doing the best one can. They

TABLE 9
How Consensual Youth Perceive Christianity

Item			No	Percentage Response Yes	?
The way to be accepted by God is to try sincerely to live a good life.	Consensual	Youth	0	96	4
	Other Church	Youth	17	60	18
Being tolerant means that one accepts all religions—including Christianity—as equally important before God.	Consensual	Youth	0	59	40
	Other Church	Youth	18	48	31
God is satisfied if a person lives the best life he can.	Consensual	Youth	0	94	6
	Other Church	Youth	15	67	16
I believe a person at birth is neither good nor bad.	Consensual	Youth	0	75	25
	Other Church	Youth	17	63	17
Salvation depends upon being sincere in whatever you believe.	Consensual	Youth	0	73	26
	Other Church	Youth	16	54	27
The main emphasis of the Gospel is on God's rules for right living.	Consensual	Youth	0	77	23
	Other Church	Youth	19	51	27
Although there are many religions in the world, most of them lead to the same God.	Consensual	Youth	0	88	12
	Other Church	Youth	16	63	19
If I say I believe in God and do right, I will get to heaven.	Consensual	Youth	0	53	45
	Other Church	Youth	35	29	31

are quite united in accepting what is variously called a folk religion, a consensus religion, or a religion in general.

It is highly significant that such youth should also be distinguished by a proclivity to prejudice. Though a cause-and-effect relationship cannot be established between these beliefs and prejudice, our data allow for the possibility by showing that the two are linked.

Another feature of consensual church youth is their expression of religious earnestness. Seventy-three percent say they have a sense of being saved in Christ, as opposed to 52% of other church youth; as "saved" youth they declare a fervency about their faith.

They express great interest in experiencing a closer relationship to God, finding meaning and purpose in life, and finding God's will for them. They say they would go out of their way to participate in activities that would help them achieve these objectives.

In spite of an avowed religiousness that is well above average, their practices of personal piety (incidence of Bible reading, private prayer, church attendance, or percentage giving) do not differ from church youth generally. Nor do they excel in sharing their faith or serving others. Their greater religiousness seems to be primarily verbal; though they use the pious words of a special relationship to the Christian faith, they lack visible evidence of a changed relationship.

Prejudice

If verbal assent to a prejudiced statement is a valid indication of prejudice, then we can say something about the extent to which it is found among church youth.

Prejudice is a respecter of age, increasing its corrosive effects to some degree as the years advance. During their youthful years people are most open to those different from themselves and least given to passing judgment on others.[2] For that reason we can expect a fairly low percentage of prejudiced church youth.

Two out of ten church youth express prejudiced attitudes (using the twenty items that assess a generalized prejudice), and three out of ten are not sure whether to agree or disagree with statements that reflect prejudice. Some say, "I really haven't thought much about it"; others who use the question-mark response are inclined to believe the prejudgment, saying, "There may be some truth in it; where there's smoke, there's usually fire."

On the average, one out of two church youth resolutely reject statements that are prejudiced, punitive in attitude, or inhumane.

Most prejudiced. A willingness to discriminate on the basis of race or color is more likely to be found among the 538 consensual youth than all other church youth. More of them will either agree with an obvious statement of bias or say they are not sure about their opinion. (We have found that question-mark answers to racial items are more likely to indicate prejudice rather than a positive attitude.)

Anti-Semitism finds fertile soil among the consensual religionists. Fewer reject obviously stereotyped prejudgments of Jews, and many more than usual hide in the woods of a question-mark response. For instance, if someone says that Jews are more likely to cheat in business, less than one-fifth of the consensual youth will agree, but two-thirds of them will declare they are not sure. Only a few agree to the comment, "Jews are not bound by Christian ethics, therefore they do things to get ahead that Christians would never do," but more than two-thirds declare their uncertainty.

There is less ambiguity in how they feel about blacks. A majority either agree or say they are "not sure" that blacks and whites should not intermingle socially. Whenever the "agree" responses are added to the "not-sure" answers on items indicating racial prejudice, there is always a majority among this consensual group.

In *A Study of Generations*, also, a strong association consistently shows up between prejudice (toward Jews, blacks, or poor people) and a religion of standards and meritorious living.[3]

> We do find bigotry and prejudice within Lutheranism, as our understanding of man, even Christian man, would suggest; however, we fail to find that prejudice is related to the belief system most central to Lutherans, namely, the Heart of Lutheran Piety. (Factor 1).
>
> Rather we find prejudice strongly connected with generalized rigidity of personality, and to a lesser extent with misbeliefs and heresies, many of which are not unique to Christianity. Church law-oriented persons, threatened by change, are prone to attitudes of prejudice; prejudiced persons are apt to cling to a law orientation (Strommen et al. 1972, p. 212).

Predictors of prejudice. The youth who are most susceptible to prejuding others are identified by certain of the thirty-nine characteristics that we tested. First and foremost is an unthinking approach to life. The strongest indicator of prejudice is the frank admission, "I seldom think about why I believe and act as I do." Apparently, education that stimulates young people to think, probe, weigh facts, and face issues is a necessary antidote to the poison of prejudice.

Ranking next is the simple acknowledgement, "My opinions on race relations are more conservative than one or both of my parents." What causes this is not known. Because it is usual for young people to be more liberal in their attitudes than parents, the opposite tendency is especially noteworthy.

The 14% of our ecumenical sample who embody the two criteria given above show by low Human Relations scores that they qualify as fledgling Archie Bunkers. They tend to place their highest value on money (plenty of money for things I want); few are bothered when they hear and see minorities abused; and a disproportionate number have low grades or have dropped out of school altogether.

Least prejudiced. Reversing the coin, we find that the *least* prejudiced youth think through what they believe and do, tend to draw excellent or above average grades, and are strongly oriented to change. For them, money tends to rank low in value and transcendental (meaning sought through relationship with others and God) values are high; most are involved in social action, along with members of their families. The least prejudiced are far more likely to know a personal caring God, but at the same time are critical of adult members for not seeming to "care."

Institutional Loyalty

Consensual youth make compliant church members. They are less likely to question what they are taught, to doubt the existence of God, or to puzzle over the divinity of Christ. They take a rosy view of the way things are. More are happy with their church (76% versus 53% of other church youth) and say they are inspired by the Sunday morning services. Fewer are critical of adult members (e.g., their stand on social issues), and fewer are ready to fault the adults' concern over or response to human need.

It is the impression of most consensual youth that adult members care a lot for each other. Seventh-three percent (versus 48% of other church youth) believe there is an openness to diversity and will cite efforts to bring together youth and adults for an interchange of viewpoints. Three out of four insist that people who are quite different (richer, poorer, another race, dress, hair) would be welcome in their church. They feel the same about how their friends would be received: "My church is interested in my age group."

The unrealistic evaluations of many seem evident in their answer to the item: "Most adults in my congregation would be able to tell you what the purpose of our church is." A total of 62% of the consensual youth say yes. Thirty-six percent of all other church youth make a similar evaluation and only 19% of one denomination's clergy make a similar evaluation. But maybe the evaluation is an accurate one from their point of view and their concept of purpose. If attending and supporting a church is a good deed, then many adult members may be quite clear as to why they are active: it is to fulfill an obligation and gain merit with God.

Loyalty to the church's youth group is abundantly in evidence for the religious achievers. A high percentage are delighted with their group, sense its progress, enjoy being with the members, and feel a real spirit of togetherness. In only one critique do they agree with church youth in general: few report an openness and freedom to share in depth some of the troubling issues of their lives. Though there is camaraderie and an esprit de corps, it is an arm's-length fellowship.

The families of consensual youth are as close-knit and religious as other church families. No more, no less. More of them, however, do admit to some racial bias in their homes. They are not free to invite persons of other races into their homes, and about half believe (or are not sure) that their families would support neighborhood efforts to keep out persons of other races.

Self-Oriented Values

The balance on values tips in the direction of self-development. Consensual youth favor goals related to their interests rather than those which seek meaning through relationships with other persons (e.g., service, ethical life, love) and with the Divine (e.g., eternal life, religion, salvation). This characteristic, however, is a weak one and cannot be stressed. It is a tendency reflected in the data and no more. Hints of this value preference appear especially for the most prejudiced youth. They tend to place high value on the acquisition of money (for things I want) and to be unperturbed when minority people are abused or treated maliciously.

Concern over National Issues

Another characteristic about which little can be said is the greater distress of consensual youth over national issues. This characteristic, too, is a weak one, and no more can be said than to identify it as a tendency. It bears mentioning, however, because it calls to mind the times when white adults have massed to protest when blacks have moved into their communities.

Summary

From the evidence supplied by a partially formed profile we can draw the following conclusions:

About one in seven church youth embody the prejudice that haunts the Christian church. They differ from other church youth in their consistent belief that acceptance with God is earned by meritorious living. They are less reflective and thoughtful and hence prone to think in stereotypes and make prejudgments. They rank lower than other church youth in academic achievement and are somewhat more self-seeking in their values. (One wonders about the degree to which intelligence accounts for these variables.)

The striking evidence that consensual youth are more likely to speak of "being saved" suggests that these youth want to talk a good game, even though they don't play an unusually good one. They believe that the successful Christian life consists of living by certain rules, coming up to certain standards; their interest in being successful at whatever they try—including the "Christian life" game—causes them to pad their scores a little. To give a testimony, to conform to certain practices, is for some a way to gain status. What they call a conversion—even though highly emotional —may be little more than a change of institutional allegiance. It lacks the change in orientation and values which accompany a profound conversion.

The Educational Process

The Christian church has a heritage of values, beliefs, life-style, and practices that center in the person of Christ. One task of parents and congregation is to transmit this inheritance and make the accumulated riches and insights of the Christian church available to young people. Passing on a faith, however, has its dangers. It can stress an orientation that has negative effects. It can require that beliefs be accepted unquestioningly, insist on ways of behaving, and draw attention away from God's intervention in the lives of men, accepting rather the dos and don'ts.

The Issue of Direction

Bel Kaufman's book *Up the Down Staircase* concerns a teacher in a New York high school who repeatedly makes the mistake of going up a staircase intended for downward traffic. The metaphor aptly describes the youth of this chapter: they are intent on going *up* a staircase of Christianity that God designed for *down* traffic. Gerhard Forde, in *Where God Meets Man*, calls this attempt to struggle upward toward perfection "staircase" or "ladder" theology. It contrasts with a faith that God comes down the staircase and gives life to people wherever they are.

Historically, Christianity has emphasized that God became incarnate in Jesus Christ and that he lived and died on earth to bring life to man. The message of the Christian church is essentially a "down staircase" story that emphasizes what God has done, is doing, and will do.

The issue in consensual youth's answers to belief items is essentially one of direction. It is not that they gave answers differing from what their church teaches, but that they attribute divine importance to their actions. This distinction is serious because prejudice is linked with an "up staircase" theology.

The Issue of Openness

In the New Testament, the Greek word for *doubt* is used in two different ways. Most frequently it is translated "to discern, to discriminate, to make distinctions, to examine, to scrutinize." In other words, doubt is a state of openmindedness wherein one sees for himself and becomes personally convinced.

This aspect of doubt is to be encouraged. Youth need a Christianity that is not a borrowed tradition, but a new life lived with conviction. The task is to provide freedom for questioning and searching, while expressing and demonstrating Christian commitment.

The positive value of openmindedness must not, however, conceal the reality of the second meaning of doubt, that of double-mindedness, the unwillingness to give oneself to God.

Some doubts are rooted, not in a need for answers, but in a need for doubts. They are traceable not to seeking the truth, but to an obstinacy of the mind, unwillingness to accept, and even hatred of the truth. It is a closed-mindedness. In this sense doubt is a sinful effort to deny God and the implications of commitment.

A good way to dissolve doubt is to hear and accept the story of who God is and therefore who we are. Faith comes by hearing this word of God. This faith in turn leads to an acknowledgment of sinfulness and a surrender to his will; it leads us to accept the God who comes "down the staircase" to man.

Openness to truth and openness to God is lacking in many youth. They do not want their stereotypes disturbed. This is precisely what the educational process must do; it must force one to question his prejudgments and boiler-plate answers to life. An educational process in home and church should teach youth to speak the language *about* faith and the language *of* faith.[4]

The language *about* faith (statements of doctrine)
   —involves generalizations about Christian truth
   —involves religious knowledge
   —expresses an intellectual perception
   —reflects a person seeking clarity of thought
   —deals with doubt directed at truths

The language *of* faith (statements which speak of what God has
   done and is doing)
   —involves statements about a living God
   —involves words of love and relationship quite unrelated to
     knowledge
   —expresses one's earnestness
   —reflects a person committed to the person of Jesus Christ
   —deals with self-doubt

I have accented the educational process of passing on truths and
Truth Incarnate because the Old and New Testaments stress this
responsibility. Furthermore, our research shows that persistent efforts at Christian education do open minds and hearts. It also
shows that the human equation—the teacher or parent—is a vital
one. When a teacher is open to God and man, when he reflects a
spirit of freedom and conviction, his pupils are drawn toward his
faith. But the parent or teacher who is occupied with no-noes
either repels the young person by his distortion of Christianity or
gains a convert for the crowd going up the down staircase.

The close link between the beliefs of youth and parents is strikingly illustrated in the study described below. Closed-mindedness
in adult parents is associated with closed-mindedness or rebellion
in their children. Faith and an openness in spirit among parents is
associated with a similar attitude in their youth.

The Issue of Parental Influence

The case has been made, through numerous research studies,
that the most significant agent in the process of religious education
is the family. When a home is characterized by congeniality, children are most likely to admire their parents and want to be like
them. When the orientation of the family is religious, the impact of
outside factors (e.g., parochial school education) may be mini-
mized except in reinforcing values the home has already established.

Using data from a 1968 national survey we tested the thesis that
congenial home atmosphere, coupled with parental religiousness, is

likely to produce youth who share the faith of their parents. To a national study of 1,000 randomly selected high-school youth (Evangelical Covenant) we added an interesting feature. A parent of each youth was asked to participate in the study in this way. As the child answered 200 survey items assessing his concerns, the parents in another room responded to the same items as *he thought his child was answering* them (neither was aware of what was being asked the other). It is assumed that if a parent and child answer similarly, this indicates a degree of closeness and understanding between the parent and youth. If the parent's answers bear no resemblance to the youth's self-report, the assumption is they are strangers to each other.

To test the similarity between the parent's and child's answers, we computed their correlation. If, for instance, a parent's answers parallel those of his child, the correlation is unity or 1. If there is no congruence between the two sets of answers, there is no correlation or 0.

We found that one parent anticipated his child's answers so perfectly that his correlation was almost unity or 1. It was .99. Some were so lacking in perception that the correlation coefficient went below 0 to a negative correlation. Their perceptions were the opposite of what the young person reported about himself.

Correlations for the 960 parents in the study ranged from −.16 to +.99. This information alone is useful because it shows why the static concept of a generation gap is a poor one. The social distance between parents and youth ranges from near to far. Some parents are unusually close to their children and show their perceptiveness in correlations above .60. Others trail off in the accuracy of their perception having no idea how their child thinks or feels.

Is accurate perception or empathy important? We chose 150 parents whose scores correlated best with their child's and 150 parents whose scores showed no correlation.

Findings. The youth least congruent with their parents contrasted sharply with those most congruent on dimensions associated with self-esteem and religious commitment. They contrasted in their beliefs, religious earnestness, personal practices or moral behavior, and degree of concern.

The "least understood" youth were less believing and less religiously earnest; they were more given to questionable practices and more troubled over personal feelings. The "most understood youth" tended to express a personal faith and a religious commitment. They also showed greater emotional stability and less inclination toward questionable or unethical practices.

What accounts for this difference? Because causation is involved, an answer cannot be given. Correlational studies can only prove the absence of causation—they cannot establish *what* causes *what*.

The data, however, support the thesis of a study which isolated two important variables in communicating a religious faith, each essential to the other. One is a congenial relationship between parents and youth, and the other is religious commitment in the parent.

Does congeniality characterize the relationship of high-correlating parents with their children?

Here is how we answered that question. When each parent and child finished the survey, he was asked to fill out a sentence completion questionnaire.

For the parent: "My relationship with my teenager (the one here) is ————."

For the child: "My relationship to my parent (the one involved in this study) is ————."

The child of one noncorrelating parent wrote: "My mother is a bitch, a snob, and a nosy Holy Roller. I despise her." The parent of that child showed her lack of perceptiveness by writing: My relationship with my teenager is ". . . a good one—we are close, and I feel she often confides in me and desires to please. We are pals."

By way of contrast note what the child of the most highly correlating parent wrote:

> I love my parents very much! Both of them. I feel they are the perfect parents. As far as my relationship is concerned, I suppose I am very close to both of them. My age (15) has probably something to do with it. The fact that I am always depending on them for everything is probably the reason I am so close to them. After

I graduate from high school and college, I *know* I will feel the same way as I do now! I have known and seen worse parents, but I can't say I've seen any better. I love my parents very much, and I have no problems they can't solve.

The parent of the child quoted above was far more tentative about his relationship. The father wrote, My relationship with my teenager is ". . . somewhat close."

These quotes, though selected, do illustrate the high association we found between a congenial relationship and the accuracy of parental empathy or perception. It would be accurate to say that a high correlation between parent and youth scores indicates an understanding parent and an open and sharing child. This becomes especially apparent in the process to be described.

We divided the parents into five groups according to the degree their survey answers correlated with their child's.

Group 1—correlations below 0 (negative)
Group 2—correlations .00 to .29
Group 3—correlations .30 to .39
Group 4—correlations .40 to .49
Group 5—correlations .50 and above.

Having read what the children of each group wrote about their relationship with their parents, we rated the quality as good, fair, or bad. A congenial relationship was considered a good one.

In like fashion, the sentence completions by parents in each group were read and rated as more or less congruent (accurate) with what the child said.

The results were fascinating. As shown in table 10 the percentage of young people whose comments reflected a good parental relationship increased steadily as the correlation approached .50 or above. They began with 42% and increased to 100%. Likewise, the percentage of parents whose answers were congruent with their child's began with 36% and increased to 100% for those with correlations of .50 or above.

In general, the higher the correlation the more likely it is that a parent resonates with son or daughter, that the youth reports a congenial or close relationship with his parent.

TABLE 10
Comparison of Family Relationships

Item	Below 0	0–.19	.3–.39	.4–.49	.50 +
			Correlation Range		
YOUTH					
My relationship to my parent is:					
Good	42%	50%	79%	75%	100%
Fair	38	29	5	10	0
Bad	21	21	16	15	0
PARENT					
My relationship with my teenager is:					
Congruent answer	36%	50%	84%	90%	100%
Noncongruent answer	64	50	16	10	0
	N = 21	N = 20	N = 21	N = 20	N = 18

One cannot assume, of course, that the accurate perception of a parent causes a cordial relationship. It can work either way. For instance, the parent whose lines of communication are open, who accords psychological freedom for his child to express himself, who has learned to listen for feelings as well as words, is best able to answer a survey "as he thinks his child is answering the items." His close relationship to his child makes it possible to anticipate quite accurately his child's thoughts, attitudes, and feelings.

It is well to note that many youth (42%) speak of a close relationship even though their parents indicate no understanding of how they feel. This suggests that there are factors other than accuracy of perception that bind youth and parents together in a good relationship. The two may be close even though one does not understand the other.

To what degree might the nature of the religious faith of parents make a difference?

To answer this question we examined the self-reports of parents regarding what they themselves actually believed, valued, and did. We noted especially the profiles and descriptive data of the 150 high-correlating and the 150 low-correlating parents. Parents, in the two groups, were very much alike in most areas under comparison (e.g., socioeconomic level, educational background, religious involvement, etc.). Where they differed markedly was in their perception of the Christian faith. Low-correlating parents tended to view Christianity as a religion of works—something one did. The high-correlating parents tended to view Christianity as a religion of grace—something one accepts as a gift.

These two types of religionists—we will call them the law-oriented (preoccupied with standards and demands) and gospel-oriented (preoccupied with promise and possibilities)—are similar to the two types of adult church members identified in *A Study of Generations* who contrast both in their perception of Christianity and in their view of people. Law-oriented parents tend to be authoritarian and overcontrolling in their approach to family life.

The differences in religious faith of the high- and low-correlating parents support the conclusion that a committed, intrinsic Christian faith is best communicated by adults who are not only accurate in their empathic relationships but also gospel oriented in their faith. In other words, openness and perceptiveness with respect to a religious faith plus an openness and perceptiveness with respect to one's children are highly associated with a similar religious faith in young people.

Postscript

This chapter has drawn attention to the tendency to live by stereotypes and prejudgments. Some youth are especially afflicted with this disease of utilitarianism, a self-centered preoccupation with advancement, security, and one's own little world. Whatever disturbs this insecure world meets the irrational response of a fearful person.

A minority of young people succumb to the disease. Fortunately, the challenge of new ideas and the stimulus of parents and teachers keep the minds of the majority alive and willing to struggle with prejudice.

A ministry to consensual youth is a serious one because many of them become the oppressors of minority people and supporters of injustice, cruelty, and racism. This ministry is grave because the dangers facing oppressors is greater than the suffering of victimized people. The suffering of minority groups does not separate them from God but the sin of the oppressor does.

A parent's or teacher's approach is not one of judgment if he believes that God has broken down the walls of hostility between all men. God loves the prejudiced as well as the sinned-against. It is this love and acceptance made incarnate in Christ that a parent and teacher must also embody in his approach to consensual youth. As indicated, the approach is educational—confronting stereotypes, stimulating reflection, and clarifying the truth of God's grace.

It's a feeling, it's a knowing,
it's a being . . . you can't define
it really.

A seventeen-year-old girl

6   Cry of the Joyous

Of the five cries of youth, one of the most insistent and frequent is
the last in the series.

Joy pulsates through this fifth cry. It may take the form of quiet
exuberance over the simple pleasures of living. Or it may be a
shout of celebration and hope that contrasts with the despair and
cynicism so often heard from twentieth-century man. It is the cry
of youth whose joy is in a sense of identity and mission that
centers in the person of Jesus Christ. As a minority group (about
one-third of all church youth), they exemplify in what they value,
believe, perceive, and do the impact of identifying with a personal
God and a believing community.

In short these youth have found a meaning system that brings
order into their lives and gives answers to ultimate questions of
existence. For them, Christianity deals with the "really real" and
supplies an explanation of "what life is all about." Their affirmation of faith, muted during the '60s, is more audible in the '70s and
may even be the most vocal cry of the decade.

Their hurrah does not always become clear with a single incident or at a first meeting. Instead, snatches of conversation, bits of
incident, moments of contact collect, and one day you realize that
they add up to a cumulative portrait of lived-out faith, persistent
joy, and hope.

Christine was like that. Not the most vivacious person in her youth group, she was often downright quiet. She was not the prettiest because, although she had lovely hair and a beautiful smile, she struggled with complexion problems. But I remember her with respect and pleasure.

I remember her in a discussion session, leaning forward in her eagerness to be understood. "But nobody ever promised us a rose garden, Pete," she said to a boy who had just spoken. "Believing that God loves you doesn't keep things from happening and hurting you. I mean, boy! When my dad was sick for so long, we were really scared we were going to lose him—I mean I had some really bad times. But, see, having faith means that you know Jesus is in there, hurting and struggling along with you. It means you're never all alone. That's a *great* thing to know."

Her look of joyous certainty was familiar. It was the reflection of an understanding of life as a precious gift, to be savored, appreciated, enjoyed, and shared.

My memories of Christine are of her responsible concern for others and patient acceptance of their quirks and oddities. Most clearly, they concern a kind of realistic optimism—hope, with its eyes wide open.

Youth Who Have Found an Identity

One winter's night, early in 1971, I sat at a table in a restaurant and chatted with a young man whose life had just been featured in a movie entitled *The Drug Scene*. It told the story of a high-school student from a middle-class home who became part of the drug culture of his community in California. His life became one of rebellion and complete separation from his high-school friends, parents, teachers, and pastor. After two years of drugs, including heroin, he was a shadow of the husky young man who once had held such promise of football prowess.

The night I talked to Mark Lindley he had fully regained his health and was looking forward to marriage and a career. What had made the difference? Through Christian friends he had been led to a commitment to Jesus Christ, and these friends formed a support group that sustained him during the painful months of reentry to freedom and responsible living. A personal faith restored his life.

There is now a new interest in the power of a personal faith because of its evident impact on the lives of so many youth. Religious conversions are radically changing the lives of some drug addicts, moving them away from personal isolation or total involvement in the addict culture into communities of faith where they become truly human persons. Authorities are coming to acknowledge that a young person's chances of becoming a delinquent, suicide, or truant depend heavily on his religious orientation and participation and that of his family. Interest is growing in the way a religious faith affects more vital and responsible citizenry.

Just as student riots and protest movements characterized the '60s, we may find, at the decade's end, that religious fervor and interest have characterized the '70s. Radical political action has given way to religious movements among college students and adolescents, few of which find their impetus from within the established church. These religious movements include the Jesus Revival, which began among the counterculture youth of California, a new Pentecostalism on Catholic and Protestant college campuses, and a revival of religious communes, all of which are part of what Jorstad describes in his book *A New-Time Religion* (1972). He calls it that because these new revival movements differ sufficiently from the religion of former revival movements to warrant a new name.

Reports on a new religious fervor in the '70s represent a marked change from the previous decade, during which religious interest was observed to be waning.[1] In the late '60s, church leaders feared for the future of the institutional church because of what seemed to be a widespread rejection of religion and its institutional expressions.

Since the data for this report were collected in the spring of 1970 and do not include youth outside the church, little of the Jesus phenomenon is reflected in the self-reports. Rather, they are a snapshot of religious interest and commitment among church youth at the climax of the tumultuous '60s.

Overall they testify to intensity of religious faith and a desire to live responsibly. The youth described here are:

—identified with a personal God,
—active with God's people,
—motivated to grow and develop.

Identified with a Personal God

A dominant characteristic of believing youth is identification with a personal, caring God. It goes beyond assent to doctrinal statements, to affirming an experienced reality. It is declaring something intensely personal—"I am convinced that God hears me, cares for me, forgives me; I have been in his presence, I have the sense of being saved, I have been heard by God." Youth who experience these realities accord great importance to their faith; it is the primary inspiration of their lives. For committed youth, Christianity is primarily a personal relationship. Though these youth are often confused on doctrinal matters and unable to distinguish between a humanist religion and the historic Christian faith, they feel identified with God. And this oneness with God is their source of joy.

> Faith is like a kite above the clouds. You can feel that exciting tug every once-in-awhile—a reassurance that he is there.
> Life in itself is a miracle and you get so excited sometimes, you flow with thanks!
>
> Jane Larson, age eighteen

The impact of a personal faith shows dramatically when the ecumenical youth are grouped on the basis of answers to the question, "How important is your faith?" The biggest difference shows in belief about God and Jesus Christ. Of those who rank faith as "unimportant," only one-fifth believe there is a God; fewer believe that Jesus is the divine son of God. This contrasts with almost nine-tenths of those whose faith is "very important."

Youth's awareness of a personal, caring God correlates with the importance that they accord their faith. The person whose faith is important to him feels quite confident that he has a personal rela-

characteristics of **committed youth**

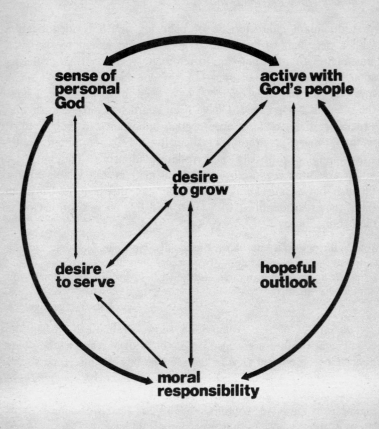

Heaviness of arrow indicates strength of intercorrelation.

tionship with God. He believes that God cares for him in a special way, that God hears his prayers, that he is being saved in Christ, that he is being forgiven by God, and that there is indeed a life after death.[2]

An identification with God is necessary for religious certainty. Though admittedly subjective, this sense of God's presence permeates all of the young person's life, affecting his attitude, behavior, and life goals. Without it he is adrift.

The survey indicates that as subjective and hidden as this feeling is, it is visible in practical, lived-out behavior. The four most typical characteristics of youth who know a personal God are these:

1. They participate actively in congregational and private religious activities.
2. They pray especially for people needing God's special help.
3. They seek God's help in deciding right or wrong behavior.
4. They reflect strong interest in help provided by the congregation.

How many in the ecumenical sample ($N = 7,050$) embody all four of the predictive characteristics given above? How many combine only three, two, or one? Answers to these questions are useful because they provide some estimate of the proportion of youth who are found in varying degrees of religious commitment.

The results are these:

76% of youth in the ecumenical sample participate actively in congregational and personal religious activities;

58% participate actively *and* pray especially for people needing God's special help;

43% participate actively, pray for others, *and* seek God's help in deciding right or wrong behavior;

30% participate actively, pray for others, seek God's guidance, *and* reflect strong interest in help provided by the congregation.

The 30% who embody all four characteristics might be viewed as the most religiously committed youth. They are the ones most conscious of God's presence and the most convinced of his love and providential care. These youth, more than all others, are eager to grow in their faith, become involved in service, and be challenged. They stand in marked contrast to the 24% whose lack of interest signals a loss of faith.

Faith does not make all of life easier; a mature perception of Christianity indicates that it isn't meant to. Our data show that a religious faith raises concerns as well as alleviating them. Distress over everyday adolescent problems does not vary with intensity of personal faith. Those who profess a faith are as bothered over lack of self-confidence, academic problems, personal faults, classroom relationships, and national issues as those who do not.

The major impact of a personal faith is seen primarily in what young people believe, value, and perceive. It affects their ethical behavior, stated concern for others, outlook on life, attitudes toward parents and congregation, and sense of personal responsibility.[3] Notable in our data is the fact that "faith-is-important" youth and "saved" youth rank much higher in self-regard. Because feelings of worth are a vital ingredient in the life of an adolescent, this is an important difference.

Active with God's People

The Siamese twin of identification with a personal God is involvement in a religious community. The two highly correlating characteristics are like two sides of a coin, answering the questions: Who am I? and, Who are my people?

Involvement, as used here, means more than church attendance. It includes being part of a religious community (attendance, financial support, membership in a youth group), taking seriously its major emphasis (Bible reading, prayer, corporate worship), adopting its basic beliefs (in God and Jesus Christ), and feeling positive about what is offered (congregational life, youth activities, and family).

The importance of religious participation and its close tie with personal faith surfaces in a multivariate analysis known as Automatic Interaction Detection (AID). In this complex computer analysis, thirty-nine possible predictors are analyzed simultaneously to determine what variables are most highly associated with saying, "My faith is important." Our analysis shows that the most powerful predictor of youth who see faith as "very important" is participation in the life of a congregation. Contrariwise, the most powerful indicator of youth for whom faith is not important is little or no participation in the life of their congregation. In other words, dropping out of congregational life is strongly associated with a diminished interest in a religious faith. Lack of involvement in a community of faith powerfully indicates disbelief in the reality of God. Though the reasons given by youth for leaving their church may be valid, it is unlikely that they are the primary reasons for their disengagement from the home congregation. It is more likely that their leaving signals a crisis in faith and unbelief.

How many youth are among the disinterested? If the answer is based upon interest in specific aspects of religious participation, then percentages will vary widely. Two-thirds of all church youth seldom, if ever, open their Bibles for private reading; nearly as many seldom, if ever, give any of their income (1% or less) to church or charity. Less than half report regularity of private prayer and participation in the church youth group. About one in five in the ecumenical sample seldom, if ever, attend church.

If all these indices of religious interest are combined into one category called religious participation, we find that one out of four of the ecumenical sample are disengaged from their community of faith and minimally identified with a personal, caring God. Three out of four touch base in some way.

For committed youth, involvement in the life of a congregation is more than performing a series of religious duties or obligations. It is being a part of a subculture that reinforces faith. It is identifying with people who, in sharing the same faith, serve as a support group. Encouragement for this interpretation is found in the contrasting life-style (attitudes, values, behavior) of youth who attend church regularly (weekly or more often) as against those who do not attend.

What does church attendance indicate? When the sample is divided on the basis of church attendance, two contrasting cultures become evident. Most nonattenders favor gratification now (e.g., premarital sex, getting high on alcohol); most attenders are willing to delay gratification. Most nonattenders place little value on charitable giving, Bible reading, or taking one's religion seriously; most attenders encourage each other in these practices. Most nonattenders criticize their church and avoid activities that would involve them in helping others; by way of contrast, most attenders are happy with their congregation and are likely to assist in helping activities.

Obviously, cultures overlap; attitudes and beliefs that typify nonattenders are found also among some attenders and vice versa. But the point is that the climate of attenders is congenial and encouraging to committed youth, whereas the climate of nonattenders is hostile and discouraging to the religious person.

Attending church is more than an isolated event in the life of church youth. It is a tangible expression of identification with a community of faith. Most regular attenders have a sense of belonging, being known, wanted, or missed. Many find their best friends at church and enjoy a sense of family when worshipping with the congregation. For them, church attendance provides occasions for fellowship. It is no surprise then that high attenders reflect a strong sense of who they are in relation to the family of God, of knowing where they belong.

Most youth who attend church several times a week are happy with their church (73%), in contrast to only 20% of the nonattenders. Eighty-three percent of the regular attenders say, "When I attend worship services, I am among friends," as against 34% of the nonattenders.

Youth group members—losers only? Some insist that youth who stay with their church, and particularly the loyal members of youth groups, are primarily "losers." They are variously seen as the "straights," the less interesting and prosaic ones. Some call them neurotics who, not being able to make it at school, huddle together in a church youth group for security purposes.

Though such generalizations may be on target for youth in some congregations, they are not so for most church youth. Comparing the 55% who attend a church youth group more than one-half the time with the 45% who do not, we find identical concerns over family unity, parental relationships, life partner, lack of self-confidence, academic problems, and classroom relationships. They are identical also in maturity of values, humanitarian attitudes, and frankness. Though participants in church youth groups are more concerned over their personal faults, they still rank higher in self-regard. There is no evidence that one group can be pitted against another on matters of personal adjustment or feelings of low self-esteem.

Where the two groups part company is in areas related to religious commitment. Large score differences show that attenders are more:

> eager for help;
> conscious of their moral responsibility;
> conscious of a personal, caring God;
> positively oriented toward their youth group and church.

Slight but statistically significant differences make it possible to add

> that attenders are more involved in social action and aspire with greater eagerness to a life of meaning and service. Non-attenders are more concerned over national issues and more oriented to change.

In summary, it is not true that regular attenders of church youth groups are less mature and more socially inadequate youth than nonattenders. If distinctions need to be made, they must relate primarily to religious interests. The distinguishing characteristic of youth who attend youth groups is the greater likelihood of religious commitment.

What are the strengths and weaknesses of today's church youth groups as perceived by the youth? If the ecumenical sample is a fair indication of church youth generally, we can say that church youth groups, compared to most organizations, have maintained a fair balance of boys and girls (46% boys, 54% girls). The youth enjoy being together and do reflect a fair esprit de corps. Primary weaknesses as perceived by the youth are these:

1. fellowship does not achieve the depths where members feel free to truly share themselves and their feelings;
2. too little is done to improve the group;
3. too few participate actively.

Motivated to Grow and Develop

A third characteristic of religiously committed youth is their strong interest in opportunities for growth and development. They are eager to participate in a range of activities offered by their church, even if it means going out of their way to do so.

Do committed youth want help?

To answer this question, we singled out the 918 youth who most resemble the profile of committed youth. We found that they, more than others in this study, want opportunities for growth in faith and service. They are, more than the rest, open to educational experiences that will enable them to be in touch more vitally with themselves, others, and God.[4]

Well-meaning adults often plan youth activities with an unrealistic stereotype of youth in mind. They do not realize that there are subcultures within a congregation, each with its distinctive interests and needs. Religiously committed youth differ markedly from nonreligiously interested young people. This is why a multiministry is essential. What strikes fire with youth having one need hopelessly bores those with another. Interest in some activities is highly related to the importance youth accord their faith.

Enormous differences in response characterizes the two groups. A youth ministry dare not plan for a hypothetical average or settle for a stereotype which assumes that all youth have similar interests and needs.

Highly committed youth declare strongest interest in opportunities that will increase their faith and their sense of identification with God and the church. Of the top seven in preference, all but two are God oriented.

First and foremost these youth, sensitive to their relationship with God, covet opportunities to enhance their sense of the presence of God. They want an increased ability to speak cogently of

TABLE 11
What Highly Committed Youth Want Most
(N = 918)

Activity	Percentage Declaring Much Interest
To experience a closer relationship with God.	93
Meetings where I experience the presence of God.	87
To learn to speak naturally and intelligently about my faith.	86
Guidance in finding out what God's will is for my life.	86
To learn how to make friends and be a friend.	81
To learn to know and understand the Bible better.	81
To find meaning and purpose in my life.	80
To experience acceptance in a group of people who really care about each other.	77
To learn to be more of the real me when I am with other people.	77
Group meetings where people feel free to say what they really think and are honest about what bothers them.	76
To learn how to be a friend to those who are lonely and rejected.	76
To learn what a Christian really is.	74
Recreation and social activities where youth get acquainted.	74
To find a good basis for deciding what is right and wrong.	72
To learn to get along better with members of the opposite sex.	72
To learn about Christian views of sex, dating, and marriage.	72
To develop greater ability to show a loving concern for others (both near and far away).	70

their faith coupled with a better understanding of Scripture. Convinced of God's providence, they want help in discerning his guidance and coming to know a life of meaning and purpose.

The next ten items in rank are relationship oriented, as seen in table 11. Their choices witness to a strong desire to make friends and be friends, to do less public posing when in a group—to be more "the real me." Committed youth want the experiential learning found in groups where members are past playing games with each other and can speak candidly about what they think and feel. Along with honesty and forthrightness, they want their group to be an accepting and caring community that also includes fun and social activity. The quality of depth interchange is eagerly desired. One touches the interests and needs of the majority of committed youth when offering the opportunities described in table 11.

Inferred Needs

Are there emphases that ought to be considered over and above the declared needs of committed youth?

Two that seem warranted from the data are: lack of conceptual clarity, and lack of orientation to change.

Cognitive clarity is not one of the dimensions that characterize religiously committed church youth in the ecumenical sample. Though they are enthusiastic about their faith, they are not able to distinguish the particularities. Though conscious of a personal, caring God who forgives them, they are not able to distinguish (cognitively at least) between a humanistic religion and historic Christian doctrines. They are as likely as uncommitted church youth to agree to statements of an American folk religion. Quite uncritically, too, the committed youth say they believe that "God is satisfied if you live the best life you can." They will assent to the statement, "Although there are many religions in the world, most of them lead to the same God."

It is quite evident that ability to make theological distinctions is not a distinguishing quality of the youthful, committed person. He is quite likely to equate Christianity with another religion, to reject a doctrine of original sin, to discount theological distinctions as "head trips," and to insist that Christianity is no more than living as Christ lived. (Here many will applaud the youth, depending, of course, on the importance they accord Christian truth.) Like new converts who are a part of the Jesus Revival, committed youth are primarily occupied with their experience of release from guilt and loneliness through knowing Christ. A teaching that harmonizes with this experience is accepted as valid.

One naturally wonders if there is any indication in the data of resistance to change among committed youth. If so, what kind of change?

First of all, they do not resist change relative to the social issues listed below. Here committed youth are as progressive in their desire for social justice and innovation as the uncommitted.

The students should have more to say about what is taught in my high school.

All war is basically wrong.

Every person has a right to free medical care if he needs it but cannot afford it.

Every person has a right to adequate housing even if he cannot afford it.

There are three changes resisted by committed youth: premarital sex, unwillingness to enter military service, and resistance to law enforcement. Of the three, change in attitudes toward premarital sex is the most adamantly opposed. Only 9% of the most highly committed youth agree that "sexual intercourse before marriage is okay as long as you love the other person." This contrasts with agreement from 35% of all others in the sample.

A second point of resistance to change is military service. Seventy percent of the highly committed ($N = 918$) feel that every young man should be willing to serve in the armed forces. This compares to 55% for all others in the sample. Greater hawkishness does not seem to be involved, however, because identical proportions of both groups (two out of three) believe that "all war is basically wrong."

Change in attitude toward law enforcement is the third point of difference. Eighty-one percent of the highly committed youth believe America needs greater law enforcement as against 67% of all others. This difference of 14% contributes to the negative correlation noted earlier as does the opposition of more committed youth to radical student activities. Only 21% agree that "the protest of college students is a healthy sign for America." This compares to 37% for all others.

To conclude, committed youth are more conservative on some

issues. In these areas one can expect a tendency to maintain *status quo* or resist change.

Finding a Life-Style

In a day of anguished alarm over what is happening in our society, it is worth noting that the life-style of religiously committed youth flows out of convictions such as these:

1. I am morally responsible for the way I live and behave.
2. I find meaning in life through relationships with others and God.
3. I believe that God is active and that my future is in good hands.

Sense of Moral Responsibility

A sense of moral responsibility is strongly associated with both religious participation ($r = .53$) and a consciousness of God's presence ($r = .55$). This means, of course, that these characteristics of religious commitment are highly interrelated even though they are separate dimensions.

This interrelatedness is seen particularly when youth of the ecumenical sample are divided on the basis of the importance they accord their faith. The committed tend to look to God for help in making ethical decisions whereas few of the religiously disinterested seek this help. For one group wrongdoing is ultimately sin against God, whereas for the other, right or wrong is only one man's opinion.

Religiously committed youth tend to feel responsible for their neighbors. This feeling of responsibility is rooted in an awareness that one's final obligation is to God and that much of this obligation is lived out in relationships with people. The obligation is to live in an awareness of other human beings, always conscious of the purpose of life. It calls each person to a sensitive awareness of his own weaknesses and alerts him to the rightful place of self-denial and sacrifice. It causes him to say:

Figure 7
How Sense of Moral Responsibility Varies
by Importance of Faith

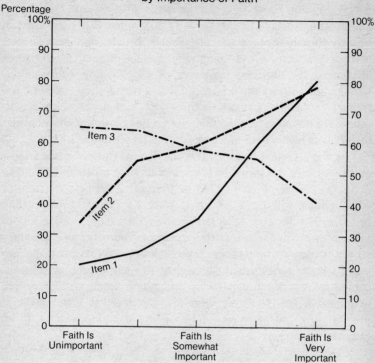

Item 1. God helps me decide what is right or wrong behavior. (agrees)
Item 2. When a person wrongs his fellowman, he sins against God. (agrees)
Item 3. What is right or wrong is only one man's opinion. (agrees)

God helps me decide what is right or wrong behavior.
When a person wrongs his fellowmen, he sins against God.

It causes him to disagree with the statement:

What is right or wrong is only one man's opinion.

This sense of moral responsibility rises and falls in relation to the importance one accords his faith.

The morally responsible person knows frequent personal, inner battles. Weighing alternatives and making choices is difficult, anxious work, but it is essential to the nature of morally responsible people. Youth know their battles well. The majority of church youth (ecumenical sample, N = 7,050) agree that they are frequently torn between conflicting values, beliefs, and desires. One of their problems is not being sure enough of their beliefs when challenged by someone. However, if they believe something is wrong, half (49%) are convinced that a friend (boy friend or girl friend) could *not* persuade then to violate their conscience. The others are not so sure. One thing is certain: church youth consider their beliefs highly determinative of what they will do.

There is a factual basis for this conviction. Current studies show that beliefs are the strongest predictors of what a person will do. In *A Study of Generations* (1972) we found that the best indicator of what a man will think or do is what he presently values and believes. For instance, the strongest predictor of a proneness to indulge in premarital sexual intercourse is the belief that premarital sex is okay if the partners love each other. What youth believe on this issue varies greatly according to their degree of religious commitment. (Because religious orientation seems so closely tied to ethical beliefs and behavior, a closer look at issues such as premarital sex, drug usage, and excessive drinking is given in an extended chapter note.)[5]

Desire to Serve

Committed youth are especially intent on finding meaning in life through relationships with others and God. In this they resemble the 2,200 children of clergymen (who were college freshmen in 1969). PKs (Preacher's Kids) who participated in the American Council on Education's Cooperative Institutional Research Program differed in some of their answers from the 250,000 incoming college freshmen of that year. They showed a greater religiosity than other students and less tendency to kick up their heels. More importantly, both sons and daughters of clergymen were more oriented toward "service" fields, tending to reject the more lucrative and prestigious fields. A larger proportion than average were also politically involved. Sons of clergymen (54% in the sample) were especially singled out for their more humanitarian attitudes and their devaluation of worldly success (Bayer and Dutton, 1972).

When church youth rank their life goals, two life-styles or clusters of behavior emerge. One places a high value on adventure, recognition, pleasure, personal freedom, and plenty of money. High priority is also given to personal power, personal physical attractiveness, and skill or expertise. All these are values strongly related to self-development.

The second life-style values a life of service, responsibility toward others, meaningful work, wisdom, honesty, a relationship with God, getting and receiving love, and knowing forgiveness and family happiness. The tendency is toward a wider life orientation.

These two life-styles or value orientations characterize church members between the ages of fifteen and sixty-five. Values of self-development are especially attractive to 76% of fifteen- and sixteen-year-olds, but remain attractive for only 50% of the twenty-three- and twenty-four-year-olds.

This suggests that self-development goals are linked to the normal process of developing a sense of worth based on personal power, recognition, skill, achievement, physical appearance, and personal freedom. Adventure, pleasure, and money can be linked to normal biological drives for "creature comforts," exploration, and gratification of instinct.

Meaningful Life. The person who endorses the cluster of life goals called Meaningful Life values relationships with others: service, ethical life, love, meaningful work, forgiveness, honesty, and family happiness. In short, he consciously endorses a value system in which meaning is found in relationships with man and God.

If all values in Meaningful Life are ranked as "least important" and all values of self-development are accorded "extreme importance," a theoretical score of 53 is obtained. If the priorities are reversed, a theoretical score of 146 is obtained. The higher the score, the more movement toward mature, meaningful values.

The average for all church youth is 115 (freshman, 113; seniors, 118). The value system of this sample of youth points in the direction of purposeful living.

The value orientation shifts for those who consider personal faith unimportant, as indicated by a score of 107. The difference between them and the religiously interested who scored 120, translated into percentiles, is 30 percentile points.

Social action. We have already seen that youth today feel the hurt of their abused fellows. More important than concern is social action: what does a person do to express his beliefs and concerns? Significantly, three out of four church youth try to reach out in a helping relationship to lonely and rejected youth. Three out of five spend time in a program of service to defend persons of minority groups and raise questions about social issues. At least half give money to people in need, identify with the suffering of others, and discuss ways in which a Christian should relate to civil rights, aging, student protest, and war.

Admittedly, there are many ways of demonstrating concern for others; there are motivations other than religious commitment for reaching out in a helping way. In this study, however, social action is positively linked to religious commitment through correlations with each of its dimensions. Though these correlations are not strong, they indicate that religious commitment is one of the motivating forces. For instance, we find that the more importance youth give their faith, the likelier is their involvement in serving activities. With increased importance of faith goes an increased sense of being one's brother's keeper.

A Hopeful and Positive Life Perspective

Committed youth tend to view their church youth group and congregation positively, to hold themselves in high regard, and to feel hopeful about the future. These attitudes can be considered characteristic along with God-awareness, religious participation, interest in help, moral responsibility, and desire for a meaningful life.

The importance of hope, eagerness, and openness to the future is best evaluated against the disillusionment, despair, and basic distrust of twentieth-century man. It contrasts with the attitudes of low self-esteem youth who feel cynical about life, separated from themselves, others, and God. It opposes peers who distrust adults and criticize all institutions, who are disillusioned with life and look to the future with despair.

Are church youth generally hopeful? A substantial majority take a positive view of the future. Almost nine out of ten believe that it is possible to make the world a better place in which to live. Eight out of ten, convinced that the future is more than a matter of luck, do look forward to becoming involved in activities which win their respect. Two out of three are convinced that good can come out of their problems and that there are many forces in life working for man. They have a sense of sharing in a great purpose. Feelings of joy and exhilaration about life characterize them.

Summary

The cry of joy that typifies one in three church youth is the overflow of a sense of identity and mission in life. Sometimes it is overpowering elation that breaks out in song; it is more usually the quiet confidence that "God walks with me, talks with me, and tells me I am his own." Its dominant characteristic is identification with a God who loves me and with a people who care about me. It is the feeling of being a whole person.

The six characteristics of committed youth show the inseparability of ethics and religion. Joined to the three characteristics of God-relationship, religious participation, and interest in help from the church are three elements of an ethical life: moral responsibility, a caring attitude, and positive outlook. For committed youth, morality is not determined by a public opinion poll; the ethical is not what most people do. Instead, it is a moral earnestness, an intentionality that includes caring for people. For these youth, a Christian faith emerges as a positive, moral force.

7 Reaching Out

You have listened to five cries and become aware of five distinct though overlapping groups of church youth. You have become attuned to five areas of need and sensitive to the way each can dominate a young person's thinking.

Though the five cries have been presented as comparable in importance and scope, it must be noted here that the first and fifth cries—self-hatred and joy—are the dominant ones. They emerge from the research (second order factor analysis) as the most intensive, cohesive, and pervasive of the five. In them one meets a classic theme of alienation and reconciliation. The first cry is one of alienation from self, others, and God; the fifth is one of identification with God, his people, and their life-style.

This fact does not mitigate the urgency of the other three cries; it only stresses a priority. Estrangement from God, a characteristic of man, leaves one restless and unhappy. Until youth come to know God as a personal, loving Father, they experience varying degrees of cosmic loneliness. Whoever reaches out to these youth must understand the loneliness that often characterizes the psychological orphan, the angry humanist, the unreflective Archie Bunker, and even the committed Christian.

Mary had been talking quietly for a long time, exploring questions about herself, her family, her life. "Sometimes I look at the stars and think how far, far away they are, and how much there is going on in the world—in the whole universe—that I don't know anything about. Then I feel awfully little—kind of nothing—but yet I know I'm not.

"Sometimes it's kind of scary just to be alive in the middle of all that. I wish I could be as sure as other kids seem to be about where they are and about what's right, and about God really being close by and helping when you have a mess in your life to work out. I'm not there yet, where I can be sure about God. I would like to be, but I'm not.

"Well, maybe that's phony, too, because I'm not sure I always would want to be asking what God wanted, if that makes sense. Because I like to see if I can do things on my own, too.

"Some kids seem to be able to think mostly about the future as being important. I keep hearing kids say, 'I'm going to be this. I'm going to be that,' but it's never 'I'm this now.' What's scary to me is the feeling that I'm never going to lose the feeling that I'm going to be . . . later on. Why isn't it important what I do now and what I am now?"

The Issue of a Cosmic Loneliness

Mary, with her sense of being "in the middle of all that," voiced the longing of many to find wholeness and significance in an overwhelming universe, to find it now. She reflected a basic lonesomeness for God, a wistfulness coupled with an admiration for friends who had found a confident faith. But lonesomeness was matched by a desire to flee God, be her own god, order her own life.

This ambivalence issues in a longing for God, mingled with fear of a God who speaks through one's conscience. The cry is one described by Augustine, "You have made us for yourself, O Lord, and our hearts can never rest until they rest in you."

In one large denomination, 63% of the youth report some degree of apartness from God and man; one-half of this group gave evidence that for them it is an acute issue. They are anxious about their relationship with God.

"I do not feel close enough to Christ."
"I wish I could have a deep faith in God."

They feel isolated from people and the excitement of life.

"I feel all alone in the world fairly often."
"I often feel as if it would be good to get away from it all."

They lack a sense of purpose; they feel that life has no meaning.

"In thinking of my life I often wonder why I exist."
"I have discovered no mission or purpose in life."

Anxiousness about God, a feeling of isolation from life, and a sense of purposelessness are indicators of a cosmic loneliness which found words in the verse which Nancy wrote in her green notebook:

> Words have many meanings
>   especially my own
> when people come to see me
>   I often turn to stone
> for when the puzzle is fitted
>   the pieces off the floor
> the picture can be recognized
>   and torn apart once more
> for in my tiny castle
>   I often sleep quite sound
> when nothing's there to bother me
>   and no one is around
> but when the winter's ended
>   (time to go and play)
> I wish that there was someone
>   that I wouldn't chase away.
>   Nancy Nelson, age seventeen

Adults underestimate the extent to which youth are anxious about a religious faith. They assume that young people are unperturbed over their relationship with God, casual about feelings of guilt, and unconcerned with doubt. Actually these are among the most disturbing thoughts of youth, outranked only by their concerns over national issues.

In the ecumenical sample used in this study, almost half (43%) strongly wish they could find a deep faith in God, and the same proportion are "much bothered" because they do not feel close enough to Christ.

A Point of View

Sociologist Andrew Greeley, in his book *Unsecular Man: The Persistence of Religion* (1972), establishes a case for man's need of an ultimate interpretive scheme that can give his life form, order, and direction. He argues that modern man, faced with persistent and overriding bafflement, even in a supposedly scientific and rational world, is caught in despair. Young people who do not know who they are, where they are going, or why they live reveal in exaggerated forms a widespread listlessness, apathy, discouragement, and frustration (Greeley 1972, p. 260). Greeley contends that drug addicts, hippies, witches and warlocks, radicals, and Weathermen are all but a tip of an iceberg of despair that comes with having nothing to believe in, no interpretive scheme, no coherence or purpose in life.

I find in my studies the same despair and sense of alienation among youth and adults who lack a faith. When we singled out the secular, change-oriented, skeptics in *A Study of Generations*, we found this same note of despair. These liberal rejecters of a faith tend to view life as meaningless, are least able to face life or death, and of all of the adult group are the most anxious about their apartness from God. The need of youth and adults for a vital Christian faith is no less today than in the past. Questions about ultimate reality continue to demand an answer.

A poignant illustration comes in the words of Brigitte Bardot, the sex symbol of the 1960s. At thirty-eight she has become a recluse with little interest in life. The Associated Press quotes her as saying, "I hate humanity. I am allergic to it. I see no one. I don't go out. I am disgusted with everything."

Unfortunately, despair is often expressed in ways that increase the alienation. Many drug users and sexual adventurers, needing the warmth and affection of close relationships, try shortcuts. They experiment with their lives, looking for satisfactions that can come only with knowledge, maturity, and personal commitment.

Girls can score just as many times as boys if they want to. I've gone to bed with nine boys in the past two years. It's a natural thing, a nice thing and a nice high. It sure can clear up the blues.

Mimi, eighteen years old

My father was always gone, and I think my mother expected too much of me. She couldn't understand, and I couldn't explain. . . . You walk around with suppressed emotions and you've got to get them out. That's the fascination of drugs; they get you out of yourself.

Bob, twenty years old

The American belief in instantaneous solutions is as widespread as the air we breathe. It is often assumed that complex mental, moral, or spiritual processes can be completed instantaneously. Tragically, the use of drugs increases this conviction.

One of the most disturbing effects of psychoactive drugs is that they convince the drug user and those around him that psychological problems have chemical solutions—that relief is just a swallow away, that better psychological living can be achieved through chemistry, rather than by coping (Rogers 1971).

Most despairing people believe that maintaining long-range ethical ideals is impossible or, at best, foolish. They do not expect future fulfillment nor do they value what lies in the future; the present moment and their current needs are overwhelmingly important.

The person who feels alienated from life is not able to postpone immediate pleasure for the sake of future gain. Along with the poor, he sees little value in setting goals for the future because of the unlikelihood of achieving them. Without a vision of the future, delay of gratification makes no sense. The despairing and alienated youth needs an answer to the question: What are the real values that are worth waiting for?

Peer-Oriented Youth

The quality of life described above intensifies the cries of self-hatred, family conflict, social protest, and prejudice. The youth for whom this is especially true are primarily peer oriented. They tend to distrust adults and take their signals from their own age group, in contrast with broadly oriented youth, who trust adults and relate well to people of all age levels.

Our studies show that a disproportionate number of peer-oriented youth hold themselves in low esteem and take a negative view of life, especially of adults. Some, psychological orphans of parents who have driven them to find refuge with their own age group, are peer oriented more through parental fault than through a preference for their own age group.

Other peer-oriented youth have left the "straight world" for ideological reasons. They flaunt traditions out of protest for the way institutions perpetuate social injustice. Others seek to escape from excessive rules and regulations; their primary goal in life is freedom from authority and imposed standards. For yet others the cause is loss of faith; in despair over not finding meaning in life they choose self-destructive paths. In *A Study of Generations*[3] we found that 18% of the church youth were peer oriented, being both antiadult and antichurch, and to some degree, involved in the life and attitudes of a counterculture.

Our data tell us that the most likely candidates for a counterculture are those who feel low self-esteem, who are pressured at home, concerned about social issues, overregulated, and alienated from God. It also indicates that though studies of American youth in 1970–71 show a strong generational consciousness and a tendency to identify with their own generation, peer-oriented church youth are a minority.

Hannsen and Paulson made a study of 210 twenty-year-olds. Half of them (N = 116) were antiestablishment subjects drawn from a random sampling of youth who entered the Los Angeles Free Clinic, a medical facility and gathering place for antiestablishment culture. The other half (N = 94) were university establishment-oriented and "straight."

The two groups contrasted strikingly in their relation to organized religion. The disaffiliation rate of the antiestablishment group was 88% as compared to 15% for the establishment youth.

How Effective Leaders Approach Youth

How does one reach out in a helping relationship to the youth described in this book?

The persons best qualified to answer this question are youth leaders who themselves excel in reaching out. In order to hear what they say, we first had to locate the cream of the crop.

Through a study conducted in 1970, we developed criteria for effective youth leaders. Once the criteria were ranked, we asked the heads of national youth organizations to nominate leaders of high-school youth who exemplify some of the highest ranked criteria.

Ninety-one youth leaders were named by the following groups: American and Southern Baptist (10); Roman Catholic (6); Christian Church (9); Church of God (9); Evangelical Covenant (7); Episcopal (4); American and Missouri Synod Lutheran (21); United Methodist (6); Greek Orthodox (2); United Presbyterian (1); and Young Life (16). The ninety-one workers then told, through questionnaires, why they intervene in the lives of youth, how they approach them, and what accounts for their effectiveness. (Note acknowledgement found as chapter note two.)[2]

Motives. The first of three questions put to the workers was: Why do you intervene in the lives of young people—that is, what contribution do you feel that you can make to their lives?

As might be expected, over half the respondents cited religious motives: "I want to share my faith," "I can guide them to a full Christian commitment," and the like.

Virtually all, in some part of their free responses, used a desire to influence youth in directions consonant with the Christian way of life as their predominant motive. And this motive clearly arose out of love, concern, and profound respect for youth.

Many responses showed that the leaders were keenly sensitive to the autonomy of youth and committed to techniques which would not violate it. Thus, they did not speak of evangelizing youth, controlling their environment, supervising their behavior, preaching the gospel to them, or other tactics that might be interpreted as applying pressure. Instead they made statements like "I can listen,"

"I can communicate," "I can be a friend," "I can be a significant adult in their lives," and "I can share my happiness."

A number of insightful youth leaders also recognized that their motivation includes self-realization. "They contribute to my goals." "They keep me young." "I can learn from them." But there was no evidence of self-aggrandizement at the expense of youth, only self-fulfillment as a consequence of helping others develop their potential.

Methods. Three questions were directed to the skills exercised by successful church youth workers. The first question was: What ways of approaching youth have you found helpful? How do you get next to them? Responses revealed six groups of skills:

1. Building Relationships
   Knowing them—home life, school, friends
   Exhibiting deep, sensitive, personal concern for them
   Showing them courtesy
   Participating with them as an equal
   Showing appreciation for a job well done
   Helping them if they ask
   Sharing mutual experiences
   Sharing my own feelings about life
2. Being Genuine
   Being adult
   Speaking in my own vocabulary
   Being honest and open
   Stating my convictions while leaving freedom for theirs
   Boldly speaking out in radical situations
   Admitting I don't know all the answers
   Dealing with my own hang-ups first
3. Being Available
   Going to their events when adults are welcome
   Spending time with them and their friends
   Working and playing with them in various activities
   Taking kids to "away" games
   Picking up hitchhikers

Inviting them to my home for dinner
Initiating interviews
4. Showing Interest
Remembering their names
Learning about their world
Being able to speak their language
Listening to their music
Adopting their symbols—beads, long hair, beard
Finding areas where I can be of help
Phone calls and letters re their accomplishments, interests
5. Communicating
Talking to them every opportunity I get
Slow, quiet listening; waiting for the chance to say some
things
Listening with the third ear for emotions
One-to-one counseling
6. Leading
Discovering and using their talents and interests
Involving them in planning, decision-making, and exe-
cuting activities
Letting them find their own thing and do it
Accepting their decisions
Face them with the issues
Holding unpopular positions which I think are best for
them
Giving them provocative, challenging books
Offering them a host of options
Presenting a better alternative by the way I live and act
Getting them interested in trips, projects, studies to bene-
fit them
Creating celebration and experiences for free expressions
Getting them to camps, retreats

The second question of this group "What are you doing to accomplish [your] purposes [with youth]?" revealed three new groups
of skills:
7. Teaching
Training others to reach out on a one-to-one basis

Training leaders to program "exposure events"

Reeducating adults to helping roles with youth

Teaching the Scripture, presenting verbally and non-verbally the message of the love of Christ

Teaching a class relating Bible, youth, and culture

Personally confronting each youth with the claims of Christ

Relating youth's ideas to Christian faith

8. Creating a Community

Helping them to get to know each other

Encouraging group awareness and sensitivity in every-day life

Finding Christ in each other, in everyone we encounter, in everything we do

Through involvement, make them aware of loneliness, deprivation, friendlessness

Helping forgiveness and acceptance to happen

Developing teamwork among youth in their activities

Trying to build a staff community

9. Encouraging Involvement

Involving kids where they can grow, experience, relate, share—volunteer work, seminars, schools, inner city, community

To Mexico yearly for service projects

Getting young people into the establishment

Creating opportunities for kids to think about, talk, act out their concerns

Discussing issues and trying to do something about them

The final question was, "If you were to describe the secret of your effectiveness, what are some of the ways of working with people that you have found effective?" It elicited no skills beyond those already revealed, but some new illustrations emerged for 8. Creating a Community: "developing groups who share at the deepest possible level" and "keeping the group open to friends of church youth."

Helping Youth into a Life of Faith

Research on Religious Development, a review of research literature on the religion of youth (1900–1969), established that adolescents who have direct personal experience of the presence of
God differ from those who do not. Our study shows in what ways
they differ: outlook on life, relations with people, motivation, and
sense of moral responsibility. It demonstrates that relationships
with God, man, and self are inextricably linked. This is why a
personal faith is deemed important by those who have it; it is why
a parent will ask, How do you help a son or daughter know a
personal, caring God?

A fitting answer is given by leaders in Young Life, an international youth organization, who underscore the necessity of first
taking the time to establish a relationship of love and trust. Once
an open and cordial relationship is established, then questions of
ultimate significance begin to surface.

"I don't know what I would do if God didn't exist. But does
he?"

"Why doesn't he make it easier for us to believe?"

The Searching Questions

It is natural for the adolescent to feel that his faith depends
upon himself, that he has to "make it" with God. And so he asks,
Am I good enough?

Assuming the negative answer, he concludes that "God is not
interested in me." Added to this concern is youth's fear of losing
the respect of admired adults. Some are embarrassed to admit to
parent or pastor that they struggle with doubts and question some
things they have been taught.

Mingled with these feelings is the wistful, unvoiced question,
"How do I 'get' faith?"

When the Bible is quoted, its words become enmeshed in the
quicksand of further doubt. "The Bible was written for people
centuries ago. By what stretch of imagination can I assume that it

speaks to me? How do I know that interpretations I make (or you make) are correct ones?"

How can the words of Scripture ever be windows through which one sees an invisible God?

Finally, because youth respond as total persons, illness, depression, fatigue, or the pressure of circumstances tend to increase their feelings of religious uncertainty.

Times of Reflection and Decision

Youth retreats, informal discussions in a home, and personal conversations provide choice occasions for helping young people think into their relationship with God and voice both their lonesomeness for God and their desire to flee him.

At times like these, young people, preoccupied with standards of right and wrong, come to recognize an issue deeper than the matter of sins, per se. It is the question of authority: Do I remain the captain of my ship, or do I acknowledge the love and authority of the God who created me?

During times of reflection and decision, youth need the freedom to discuss the mystery of their rebellion and their proneness to go it alone. One can only encourage them to remain open to God's voice, allow times for listening, and take advantage of moments when he can be heard.

These are not times for a hard sell or for "thought-terminating cliches" which can force an artificial conversion that is mere acquiescence to a religious culture, without knowledge of the love and grace of God.

Youth need to understand that Christianity is a relationship with Christ, in which doubt is admissible because one relates to a person and not to a set of doctrines. Accepting a personal, caring God comes first; in coming to know him, one learns what is embodied in propositional truths.

When youth hear what God has done in the past and can do again for them, conversations about God become hope-inspiring occasions. Youth's attention shifts from themselves and their problems to the promises and possibilities of the Christian faith. The emptiness of a lonely life and the drawing power of love implicit in God's promise motivate them to enter God's possibilities as a child returns to his father's arms. In receiving a Savior, youth come to a personal transcendental experience with Jesus Christ.

A Supportive Congregation

A personal faith needs the sustaining power of a group. But what can give youth a sense of welcome and identification with his congregation?

Of the thirty-nine possibilities tested, two were highly associated with positive, warm feelings toward one's congregation: the first, to feel that one fits in well with some group in the congregation; and the second, to feel inspired at worship services.

It is hard to overemphasize the identification youth feel with their congregation when they are secure in a small group. If the youth interact first even in discussion groups of twelve to fifteen people, they later find the freedom to share themselves in the larger group.

An enigma for youth is why gatherings to celebrate their faith, such as Sunday morning worship, are often dull. Many find inspiration totally lacking in this function of their church family.

TABLE 12
Percentage Inspired by Local Worship Services
Ecumenical Sample
(N = 7,050)

	Percentage Saying Yes
A. Never inspired, only bored	11
B. No longer inspired, but I once was	11
C. Very often inspired	13
D. Quite often inspired	17
E. Sometimes inspired	32
F. Seldom inspired	15

Unlike adults, youth today are conscious not only of God's transcendence but also of his immanence. They look for more than a service that stresses his holiness, transcendence, and awesome greatness. They want more than the solemn beauty of a service where architecture, music, and liturgy create the sense of God's presence. Youth also want to worship the God who sits next to them in the fellowship of believers.

Youth want to worship a Christ, not only divine but also human, who is a part of rhythm, melody, and ordinary speech. They want a service that inspires, encourages, and helps them to feel what they are unable to make themselves feel.

One group of youth, after several weeks on the issue, agreed on three things they want in a morning worship service. First, it should be a time of singing, of expressing happiness over what God has done and is doing. If a service does not lift one's spirits, why speak of Good News?

Second, they want to learn something new and be stimulated intellectually by fresh insights into Christian truth.

Third, they want to participate and meet God in the presence of others. They want the service to impart a sense of warmth, love, and community.

A Stance toward Youth

Though this book is written for parents and youth leaders, it should not be assumed that adults have outgrown youth issues. On the contrary, the preceding analyses show how much adults are linked to youth needs.

Low self-esteem is probably passed on from parents.

Family disunity centers in parental conflict.

Social concern is characterized by youth's sharp criticism of congregational adults' lack of manifest caring.

Prejudice is found more readily among adults than among youth.

Loss of faith is an issue that is no respecter of age.

A ministry to youth is best seen as a collaborative effort— mutual seeking, helping, and working—in which adults freely admit their need to be helped in ways similar to youth. To believe that "no one has arrived" enables everyone, regardless of age or experience, to express the need for rebirth or renewal, for judgment and forgiveness.

The stance of common need reduces the age prejudice that characterizes most adults and mitigates the generational chauvinism of youth who feel superior to adults in such personal values as openness, honesty, and feeling for people.

It does not require that young people be seen as little adults. One can still view adolescents as possessors of special qualities—liveliness, enthusiasm, honesty, idealism, and potential—and rightfully say, "I enjoy them," "They keep me young."

The preceding chapters draw attention to at least two imperatives in a youth ministry—*mutuality* and *mission*. Youth of all subcultures want the warmth of an accepting group which is *mutuality*. They need activities which give them a sense of purpose; that is *mission*. Within these two polarities, there is powerful need for *educational experiences* for youth and adults that open minds, develop skills, clarify values, and encourage commitment.

Notes

1. To Hear and Understand the Cries

1. When the correlations of youth's answers to the 420 items were analyzed, the items formed twenty-five clusters. These in turn were subjected to a second order factor analysis in order to derive the five sets of characteristics.

2. The five sets of characteristics (factors) that provide the structure and documentation for the chapters of this book are listed here. The nature of each group is established by the characteristics which load most heavily (i.e., highest numbers).

FACTOR ONE—LOW SELF-ESTEEM
Positive Loading

87	Personal Faults (concern over)
81	Lack of Self-Confidence (concern over)
79	Classroom Relationships (concern over)
64	Academic Problems (concern over)
61	God-Relationship (concern over)
58	Life Partner (concern over)
51	Lack of Family Unity (concern over)

Negative Loading

− 52	Self-Regard

FACTOR TWO—FAMILY CONFLICT
Positive Loading

73	Family Pressures
66	Parental Relationships (concern over)
63	Lack of Family Unity (concern over)

Negative Loading

− 51	Family Social Concerns (perception of)

FACTOR THREE—SOCIAL-ACTION ORIENTATION
Positive Loading
69	Human Relations (Humanitarian Attitudes)
62	Orientation for Change
59	Involvement in Helping Activities
46	National Issues (concern over)

Negative Loading
− 42	Congregational Adults as Caring (perception of)

FACTOR FOUR—CLOSED-MINDED
Positive Loading
42	Family Social Concern (perception of)
40	Congregational Adult Caring (perception of)
36	Church Youth Group (perception of)
33	National Issues (concern over)

Negative Loading
− 61	Biblical Concepts
− 30	Human Relations (Humanitarian Attitudes)

FACTOR FIVE*—RELIGIOUS COMMITMENT
Positive Loading
82	Religious Participation
79	Awareness of a Personal God
68	Interest in Help
67	Sense of Moral Responsibility
54	Desire for Meaningful Life
54	Church Youth Group (perception of)
44	Congregational Adults as Caring (perception of)
43	Involvement in Social Action
32	Self-Regard

3. Our data provide additional information about families of church youth, as well as information on school and leisure-time activities.

Family. In the ecumenical sample three out of four youth (78%) report that both parents belong to the same congregation and nine out of ten say that at least one parent belongs to a church. The religious earnestness of these parents is not known except to say that in 14% of the homes family devotions or prayers are held regularly.

One-fourth (26%) of the main wage earners are in a profession (doctor, lawyer, teacher, minister, etc.), and three in ten (29%) are in sales or business activities. In addition to these white-collar workers, 20% are in skilled or unskilled manual work, 6% in farming, and 4%

* Though listed here as the fifth factor, it follows Factor One in strength and intensity.

in a service occupation (e.g., barber, waiter). New occupations, technical or scientific, account for 14%. These percentages indicate that more youth in the ecumenical sample come from white-collar homes than in the total population of American teenagers.

This difference in socioeconomic status is reflected also in the educational level of the parents. Fifty-one percent of the fathers and 41% of the mothers have had at least some college or university work. This is well above the average of 24% for Americans aged 35 to 44, 19% for Americans aged 45 to 54.

Families of church youth are larger than the national average, with half the youth in the ecumenical sample reporting three or more brothers or sisters. No more than one in ten is an only child. The families are well established in their communities; no more than 15% have moved during the past five years. (Note well: the high mobility rates for Americans are related to age: 46% of Americans ages 20–24 move annually and also 38% of the 25–29 age group. In 1969–70, 18% of all people in the United States changed residency.)

Stability of home life is shown by the fact that a majority of the church youth do not report difficulties and stress in their homes. Divorce or separation is known by one in ten (8%), and frequent illness, by only 10%. Around three in ten of the youth (29%), however, are conscious of financial troubles in their homes, and about as many report serious difficulties such as prolonged illness, unemployment, death, injuries, or personal problems. Around one in four have trouble getting along with father (27%) or mother (25%), and 21% acknowledge that father is seldom home. In 43% of the homes, mother is employed one-half to full-time—a percentage similar to the national average.

School and leisure. Over half the ecumenical sample describe their grades as above average (42%) or excellent (11%). Less than one in ten admits to below average (7%) or very low grades (2%). Church youth have the ability to do well in school. Apparently they have the motivation as well; three out of four are never absent or, at the most, miss school once per month.

The ecumenical sample has a higher percentage (24%) than average of youth who attend a religiously sponsored parochial school. Private and technical schools account for another 7%, leaving a total of 67% who attend a public school. Only 1% are dropouts.

When it comes to leisure-time activities, averages become misleading. A fifth of the youth (18%) are gone five to seven evenings per week from their home, and the same number are seldom gone (one evening or less). Though television is readily available, only one in five (20%) watch TV sixteen hours a week or more, and they show similar profiles to those who seldom watch it. If excessive TV watching constitutes a problem, it ranks in significance well below the issues posed in this report.

4. Margaret Mead contends that events between 1940 and 1970 have ushered in a new age. Today's youth, she says, are natives of this new world and are to adults like the advance guard of an invading army—strangers. She believes that between generations a break has occurred which is wholly new to history—a break that is planetary and universal.

In general, Margaret Mead distinguishes three kinds of culture:

Post-figurative, in which children learn primarily from their forebears;

Co-figurative, in which both children and adults learn from their peers; and

Pre-figurative, in which adults learn also from their children.

Post-Figurative Culture

According to Mead, this is the isolated, primitive culture where one finds three generations: Grandfather, father, and son. One rears his children as he was reared; he teaches what he was taught. The underlying assumption is that youth accept unquestioningly what is unquestioned by the adults. As a result, there is considerable conformity to, and replication of, the past.

I was conscious of three-generation families when visiting Norway in the summer of 1971. In the homes I visited, the grandparents were honored people whose opinions were respected. They served as links to the traditions of the past and gave the children a sense of history. If there was generational tension, it showed in youth's reactions to their parents.

Co-Figurative Culture

In the co-figurative model, both children and adults learn from their peers. Contemporaries are the strongest influence on individual behavior, whether this behavior involves adults or youth. The style of life and the limits, however, are established by adults. It is a pattern of life where people of two generations share with each other.

Co-figuration occurs when the experience of one generation is radically different from the preceding generations, as for example when youth emigrate to a new land and encounter new situations and new ways of handling them. Youth of this culture, though reared to expect change, understand that it is change within the changeless. It is assumed that, in spite of change, they will retain their cultural identity, and everyone knows and agrees on basic values. In such a culture it is possible for radical groups to become champions of the past and to institutionalize their values. One can assume that in the co-figurative culture there is tension between the past and the changing present.

This pattern may exist in church life where adults collaborate with youth in partnerships in which coseeking, cosharing, and coworking are mutually enriching.

Pre-Figurative Culture

In Mead's opinion, today's youth are part of a new culture. Underlying it is an assumption that nothing in the past is meaningful or workable and that one can learn very little from adults.

This new culture proclaims that existing social structures must be torn down to make way for radically new approaches to critical world problems. Social bulldozing is required, says Margaret Mead. It is assumed that adults cannot teach *what*, but only *how* to learn. Youth do not want to be told *what* to be committed to, but only the value of being committed to something.

In this culture, a relationship of trust between adults and youth must be established along with a new life-style. Though adults will be needed to supply the know-how and stability, the youth can point out the needs and the opportunities for cooperation-building.

Mead believes that primitive societies and small religious ideological groups are primarily post-figurative; that great civilizations like ours have adopted co-figurative learning as a technique of incorporating change; and that we are entering a period, new in history, in which the young take on authority in their apprehension of the unknown future.

We tested Mead's "radical break" theory by using statements taken directly from her writing in a survey of Lutherans ages 15–65, *A Study of Generations*. If her claims that today's youth are a new breed are correct, we can expect that Lutheran youth will choose quite exclusively the statements of a pre-figurative point of view. Also we can expect adults to reject pre-figurative statements and choose only co-figurative or post-figurative points of view.

POST-FIGURATIVE

Life is unchanging and will continue largely as I know it.

The accumulated wisdom of the past should be one's primary source of learning.

Young people learn primarily from their forefathers and elders.

I have accepted unquestioningly what was taught by my elders.

CO-FIGURATIVE

Though life is constantly changing, human nature and human ideals do not change.

What is currently being discovered and what men have learned in the past are about equally important to learn.

Young people learn primarily from participating with adults and youth together.

Conflict and change have forced me to rethink and restate ageless truths for myself.

PRE-FIGURATIVE

Life has changed so radically that youth and adults cannot understand each other.

The past is such a colossal failure that there is little or nothing from the past worth learning except know-how.

Young people learn primarily from their own age group (peers).

I have questioned everything from the past and, together with my own age group, have sought new approaches to life.

Approximately two out of three youth preferred co-figurative to pre-figurative responses. The same proportion of adults also preferred a co-figurative position. Only 21% of the youth, ages 15–20, chose the pre-figurative statements, as against 15% of the adults, ages 30–65. The difference of 6% is too slight to be significant, and certainly does not warrant talk about a radical break between these generations.

If, on the other hand, we see Mead's typologies as world views that are favored by one age group more than another, then we have supporting, though weak, evidence. Most likely to agree to post-figurative statements are people 50–65 years old (19%), and most likely to agree with pre-figurative statements are the youngest, ages 15–18 (24%).

One can look at Mead's theory as a prediction of the future and consider it an interesting hypothesis. Viewed in this light, her analysis is both provocative and instructive. We may, in fact, see more of the pre-figurative mode in the years which are to come. A shift in perceptions, values and attitudes toward adults may be in process. But there is little evidence that such is the case now, at least as far as church youth are concerned. To talk about a new breed when referring to this population is to propound a myth.

2. Cry of Self-Hatred

1. A separate sample was drawn of young people who most resemble the profile of low self-esteem youth. They score in the top quarter on Personal Faults and Lack of Self-Confidence and in the lowest quarter on Self-Regard. The penetrating quality of loneliness became

apparent through a multivariate analysis (Automatic Interaction Detection) of the data. This method was used to identify the elements in a young person's life that most powerfully predict self-esteem (the scale, Self-Regard, being used as the dependent variable). Thirty-nine possibilities were examined simultaneously to determine which accounted for the most variance of self-regard. Of the thirty-nine possibilities used as independent variables, the one ranking first was the item, "I tend to be a lonely person," meaning, the most powerful predictor of youth who hold themselves in low regard is their admission of continuing loneliness. Ranking second to loneliness was the statement, "I sometimes consider suicide." This means that when the dimension of loneliness is controlled (i.e., its effect or impact is kept constant) then thoughts of self-destruction are most indicative of low self-regard.

2. Unpublished paper presented at the International Congress of Learned Societies in the Field of Religion, Los Angeles, California, 1972 by Drs. Peter Benson and Bernard Spilka, University of Denver.

3. Figure 8 shows how the population of 7,050 youth divides when analyzed by means of an AID (Automatic Interaction Detection) program. Thirty-nine contributors to low self-regard were processed simultaneously against the dependent variable, Self-Regard. This process locates the most powerful predictor of self-regard (the dependent variable). Having divided the sample on that predictor, it locates the second strongest variable and divides the sample again. The three contributing most to self-regard (and which, therefore, can be called predictors) are these:

1. Being less critical of oneself
2. Not considering suicide
3. Enjoying high grades

The strongest predictors of low self-regard (in order of importance) are these:

1. Being highly self-critical
2. Considering suicide
3. Considering one's faith unimportant

The concept of esteem may not be measured simply by isolating one dimension—Self-Regard. Therefore another analysis was carried out using self-criticism (Personal Faults) as a primary focus. Again a multivariate analysis was used to determine the proportions of youth who report high or low self-esteem.

Of thirty-nine possible contributors to a self-critical attitude, the two most powerful predictors turned out to be: high concern over classroom relationships and extreme concern over one's lack of self-confidence. Using these as prime indicators of low self-esteem, we can say that one out of five (20%) are troubled in these ways. This is an

Figure 8
Major Predictors of Self-Regard

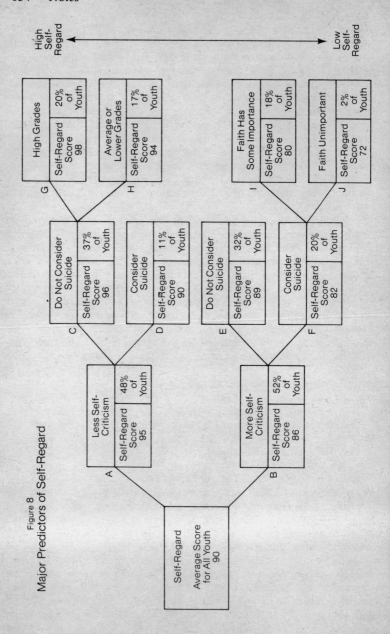

identical percentage that resulted when Self-Regard was used as the basis for the multivariate analysis.

4. Parent Effectiveness Training is a course in which parents learn the essentials of good two-way communication. Its founder, Dr. Thomas Gordon, heads Effectiveness Training Associates, a nationwide network of professionals offering training programs for parents, teachers, counselors, youth workers, and organizational leaders and administrators. Headquarters are located at 110 South Euclid Avenue, Pasadena, California 91101.

Further description of P.E.T. is found in chapter 3, chapter note 5.

3. Cry of Psychological Orphans

1. The predictive power (actually 35) of the item "My father and mother do not get along" is due in part to the fact that the item is also a part of the scale, Family Unity, that serves as dependent variable. Table 13 shows other powerful predictors of family disunity.

TABLE 13
Predictors of Family Disunity

Items	No. of Times More Predictive of Family Disunity, Than Separation or Divorce
My parents do not trust me.	19
My parents nag me.	16
My parents try to pry into my private life.	16
My parents do not understand my dating problems.	16
My parents do not let me make my own decisions.	15
It is hard to discuss my problem with my mother.	14
My parents are too strict.	14
My parents seem to have forgotten how it feels to be young.	13
I have trouble getting along with father.	12

2. A multivariate analysis using thirty-nine predictors with the Family Unity Scale as the dependent variable identified the three most powerful predictors of Family Unity. Figure 9 shows how the population of 7,050 youth divides on the basis of three variables: parental accord, parental trust, and open communication. Concern over family unity drops from an overall average score of 46 to 36 to document the change in climate when parents get along. It drops again (indicating

less concern over unity) to 29 when the second predictor, namely parental trust, shows its influence by dividing the sample. Though third in rank, the importance of open communication is also evident in the scores. For youth who find it hard to discuss their problems with mother, the Concern Over Family Unity score moves up from 29 to 35.

3. Parents involved in helping activities enjoy homes marked by unity, good parent-youth relationships, and a minimum of pressures. The opposite is also true. A consistent negative correlation varying between .30 and .33 exists between Family Social Concerns and the other three family characteristics (Family Pressures, Parental Understanding, and Family Unity).

4. Division of Youth Activity, The American Lutheran Church, 422 South 5th St., Minneapolis, Minn. *Parent/Child Covenant Theatre.* May, 1971.

5. Following is a brief description of what is taught in Parent Effectiveness Training (P.E.T.) classes:

Parents are taught to differentiate situations in which the child is having trouble meeting his own needs as a person and those in which the child is making it difficult for the parent to meet his own needs.

Parents are given skill-training in those forms of verbal communication shown to be most effective in helping another person overcome difficulties in meeting his own needs. They are actually taught the particular forms of communication utilized by competent professional counselors, such as "reflecting feelings" or "active listening" (from Carl Rogers and other client-centered therapists), empathic "open-ended questions," and methods of keeping the responsibility for problem-solving in the hands of the child.

They are taught ways to influence the modification of the child's behavior that is interfering with the parents' needs. These methods have low probability of producing guilt and resistance and high probability of maintaining the other's self-esteem. P.E.T. thus teaches parents to send "congruent" messages (from Rogers), to be "transparently real" (from Sidney Jourard), to confront the child with "I feel . . ." messages, and to keep the responsibility for the problem with the parent who actually owns it.

Another aspect of training concerns specific methods of preventing conflicts between parent and child, such as enriching or modifying the child's environment, preparing the child ahead of time for change, and conducting participative decision-making meetings for setting rules and policies that will govern the child's behavior in future situations.

Throughout, parents learn the harmful effects of using either of two "win-lose" (power-struggle) methods of conflict resolution—Method I (parent wins and child loses) or Method II (child wins and parent

Figure 9
Predictors of Family Unity

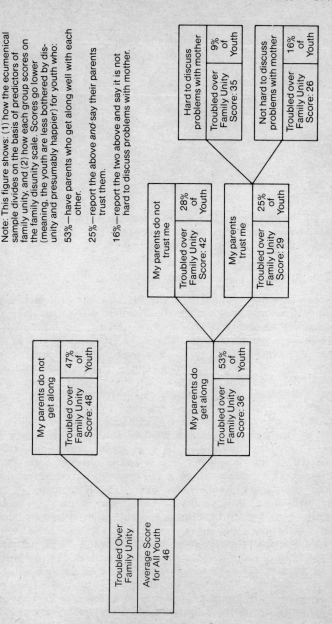

Note: This figure shows: (1) how the ecumenical sample divides on the basis of predictors of family unity, and (2) how each group scores on the family disunity scale. Scores go lower (meaning, the youth are less bothered by disunity and presumably happier) for youth who:

53%—have parents who get along well with each other.

25%—report the above *and* say their parents trust them.

16%—report the two above and say it is not hard to discuss problems with mother.

Troubled Over Family Unity
Average Score for All Youth
46

My parents do not get along
Troubled over Family Unity Score: 48
47% of Youth

My parents do get along
Troubled over Family Unity Score: 36
53% of Youth

My parents do not trust me
Troubled over Family Unity Score: 42
28% of Youth

My parents trust me
Troubled over Family Unity Score: 29
25% of Youth

Hard to discuss problems with mother
Troubled over Family Unity Score: 35
9% of Youth

Not hard to discuss problems with mother
Troubled over Family Unity Score: 26
16% of Youth

loses). A nonpower or "no-lose" method of resolving conflicts is taught in which parent and child mutually search for an acceptable solution making it unnecessary for the parent to force submission on the part of the child (Gordon 1970).

6. Youth-Reaching-Youth, known as Project YOUTH, was conducted by Youth Research Center, Minneapolis, under a grant (#MH17615-01) from the National Institute of Mental Health.

7. The program especially successful in developing a strong support group and effecting the above changes is available in the publication, *PEER Program For Youth*, by Ardyth Hebeisen, Augsburg Publishing House, Minneapolis, 1973.

4. Cry of Social Protest

1. The sample of 335 socially concerned youth was drawn from those who scored in the top quarters of the Human Relations, Orientation to Change, and Social Action scales.

5. Cry of the Prejudiced

1. The nature of the religiosity of the committed and consensual orientations may be more specifically inferred from the defining characteristics of each coding component. Briefly, the individuals in the Committed group conceptualize religion (content) largely in terms of abstract principles, intangible ideas, and relational expressions. They seem to order these concepts and express religious ideas with relatively clear meaning and nonambiguous referents (clarity). They also apparently distinguish and delineate a relatively large number of religious categories, characteristics, and functions using multiplex rather than global or overgeneralized ideas (complexity). Such individuals further order these complex, abstract religious concepts discerningly and express their religious ideas clearly (clarity), examining and considering different or similar opinions, beliefs, and practices in a straightforward manner. This indicates an open and relatively accessible religious outlook (flexibility). Religion, for this group, is a matter of personal concern and central attention; the emotional commitment to religious ideas, ideals, and values seems to account for, or at least be relevant to, daily activities (importance).

By contrast the religiosity of the individuals in the Consensual group appears to be more tangible and literal. Practical, observable referents and concrete, graspable images are preferred to abstract, philosophical ideas (content). Their view of religion is apparently vague, obscure, and indistinct in meaning and reference as reflected in "conventional" statements, vague generalizations, and amorphous, subjective impressions (clarity). While their religion is composed of a relatively small number of categories or elements, these are typologized and global with a tendency to use dichotomous or bifurcated categories and to evidence "two-valued" logic (complexity). Such a religion is relatively restrictive or closed to differing ideas and practices in that these individuals apparently try to narrow or encapsulate religiosity by rejection and distortion, or by an "insistence" on appropriate ideas, proper behavior, and "right" beliefs. Such diversity-intolerance may also minimize perceived differences within their own belief system as well as generating a nonaccessibility through various "screening" techniques (flexibility). Lastly, the religion of such individuals tends to be detached and neutralized. While considered important, it appears severed from substantial individual experience. It might also reflect an emotional "clinging" or magical quality, or be neutralized and attenuated by other concerns or lack of positive affect and identification, thus rarely influencing or being involved in daily activities and behavior (importance) (Allen and Spilka, 1966).

2. Age and education are strongly related to prejudice. A careful charting of their effects on church members from ages 15 to 65 are found on p. 209, *A Study of Generations* (Strommen et al. 1972). Prejudice scores, lowest for youth, tend to rise with advance in years. However, graduate trained adults, including clergy, do not score higher with age, until they reach age 50.

3. In *A Study of Generations* a major finding was the discovery of a prominent life-orientation to rules and regulations among church members. A profile of this orientation consists of sixteen characteristics, of which the following are the most dominant. They cannot tolerate change, have a need for religious absolutism, are prejudiced, are threatened by people different from themselves, are self-seeking in their relation to religion, and believe in salvation by works.

These characteristics parallel the classic theological descriptions of a *law*-oriented person. Therefore, we assume that the underlying quality uniting the constellation of sixteen characteristics can be called, in theological terms, a law-orientation.

An illuminating treatment of prejudice among church members is contained in James Dittes book, *Bias and the Pious*, published by Augsburg Publishing House, Minneapolis, 1973.

4.. Distinctions made by Dr. Paul Holmer, Yale Divinity school.

6. Cry of the Joyous

1. Douglas Heath, through his twenty-year-study (1946 to mid-1960s), concluded that "the religious way of life, as manifested in traditional forms and beliefs, has been gradually losing its appeal." He

noted that the religious beliefs, values, practices, and attitudes of the '60s are much less orthodox than those of youth in the late '40s and '50s. A similar conclusion is given by a study of religious change among college students over two decades. Hastings (1970) noted that the main changes were diminished traditional religious commitment, liberalization of beliefs, diminished religious behavior, more and earlier religious questioning during adolescence, and fewer designations of religious preference.

2. The God-Awareness scale, a dominant dimension in the factor of religious commitment, served as the prime indicator of religious commitment. A computer analysis ran thirty-nine independent variables against this scale, or dependent variable, to determine what contributes most to youth's awareness of God as a personal, caring father. The purpose is to determine the relative impact or contribution of each of the thirty-nine variables. The four contributing most are singled out as the most powerful predictors of a high or low awareness of God as a personal, caring father.

The analysis shows that 30% of the youth in the ecumenical sample can be classified as committed youth with the rest of the youth reflecting varying degrees of religious commitment or the lack of it.

The unique contribution of this approach to data analysis is twofold: (1) insight into the structure underlying youth's awareness of God; and (2) an estimate of the proportions of youth found in each subcategory. Here are the conclusions that seem warranted:

Conclusions on Degrees of Religious Commitment

1. Three out of four (76%) of the ecumenical sample (N = 7,050) are sufficiently involved in the life of their congregation to be identified as churchmen and women.
2. Of these, 18% are not given to praying for others in need of God's help. Their diminished identification with God is symbolized by some (6%) who do not believe in a personal God. They are youth who participate actively in their church, but lack a personal identification with God.
3. More than half the youth (58%) are involved in their congregation and pray for people needing help.
4. Of these, a total of 15% do not seek God's help in deciding what is right or wrong behavior: some (2%) because they do not believe in a personal God, and others because they are not sufficiently conscious of God to be seeking his help. A few may consider it none of his business.

   Here, too, are active churchmen whose sense of a personal God is vague and unreal.

5. Two out of five (43%) church youth are keenly aware of God's presence (God-Awareness score = 116). They pray for others in need of help and seek God's guidance as to what is right or wrong.

6. The most religiously committed youth are the 30% whose heightened awareness of a personal, caring God is reflected in both their score (119) and in their strong interest in congregational activities.

7. Somewhat less committed youth are the 13% who take their faith seriously, but seldom participate in the supplementary offerings of their congregation such as group meetings, youth activities, and special meetings. They show little or no interest in opportunities for growth and development and are less conscious of God's presence and help (score 110).

8. There are varying degrees of piety and confusion among the nonparticipants (24%) in a congregation. A third (8%) will admit to praying for others in need. The others who are not so inclined (16%) have among them a number who reject the idea of a personal God. But, oddly, even among these there are the contradictory few (3%) who still seek God's help in deciding what is right or wrong behavior.

9. Among church youth a hard core of 5½% consistently reject a personal God. Four independent measures show that their alienation from God is both conscious and unequivocal.

10. Religiously committed youth are ones who:
   are involved in a community of faith;
   pray for people needing God's help;
   seek God's aid in deciding what is right or wrong behavior;
   show interest in opportunities for growth.

3. Table 14 shows how declared Importance of Faith relates to dimensions of values, beliefs, and perception.

4. To determine the top-ranked interests of committed youth, the following procedures were used. All who scored in the top quartile of three dimensions (God-Awareness, Religious Participation, and Moral Responsibility) were singled out as religiously committed youth. The discussion which follows on help wanted by highly committed youth is based upon the percentage of these 918 youth who said, "I am very much interested and would go out of my way to participate" in this activity. (Note: a fairly strong association has been found between declared interest and actual participation. Also it has been found that these items separate the religiously interested from the religiously disinterested youth. Highly motivated religious youth, e.g., youth group officers, usually tend to choose many activities and declare strong

TABLE 14

Relative Importance of Faith

Scale No.	Dimension	Average Standard Score		Difference* in Standard Score
		Faith Important	Faith Not Important	
10	God-Relationship	50	45	5
11	Interest in Help	53	43	10
14	Moral Responsibility	53	43	10
15	Meaningful Life	53	44	9
16	Religious Participation	55	38	17
17	Social Action	52	45	7
18	Self-Regard	52	47	5
20	God-Awareness	54	40	14
22	Youth Group Vitality	52	46	6
23	Adult Caring	52	45	7
24	Family Social Concern	52	46	6
		N = 4208	N = 761	

* All differences are significant at a .001 level.

interest. Youth, on the other hand, who rarely attend a religious service choose very few.)

5. Use of these three topics does not mean that moral responsibility is no more than avoiding intercourse, drugs, and alcohol. The 1973 Watergate trials involving perjury, theft, invasion of privacy, and dishonesty of high-placed people reminds us that far more is involved. What follows is being shared because it is available data and because it shows how a sense of responsibility in matters of gratification is related to a faith commitment.

Is premarital sex considered okay? Well over half (56%) of the ecumenical sample of 7,050 young people are bothered to some degree because they allow their feelings to overbalance their values in matters of sexual behavior. The battle of conscience, however, is more than keeping one's feelings under control. For half the population of church youth, the problem is also a matter of being able to explain what they believe and why. They find it hard to defend their moral beliefs, to explain why they believe premarital sex is not okay even when it is an expression of love.

Statistics do not give answers to moral issues, but they can describe the youth who hold certain moral beliefs.

Some who believe that premarital sex is okay reflect exemplary credentials. They know a sense of purpose in life, believe they are "saved," are concerned about others, are active in their congregations, chaste while on a date, devout, and conscious of God's guidance. These, however, are a small minority. The much larger number reflect a stance toward life that is antithetical to Christian commitment. They tend to hold beliefs, values, attitudes, and life-styles that are self-serving and hedonistic.

The interrelationship of this belief with an unwillingness to delay gratification is seen when the sample is divided on the basis of response to the statement: As long as you love the other person, sexual inter-course before marriage is okay. The percentages given below indicate the number for whom sexual intercourse on a date is something considered possible—that is, an issue that poses a personal battle.

Of those who respond to "Premarital sex is okay"		This percentage will consider sexual intercourse on a date
Strongly disagree	34	4
Disagree	32	10
Agree	23	24
Strongly agree	9	37

Similar increases appear when the issues are drug usage, getting high on alcohol, or theft.

Premarital sex is okay	Have Used Drugs	Sometimes High on Alcohol	Have Taken Things
Stronglv disagree	6	16	42
Disagree	11	27	51
Agree	22	47	64
Strongly agree	37	56	69

These youth favor chastity but for different reasons possibly than those of past years. The fear-oriented approach of yesteryear is giving way to more positive and goal-oriented controls. Young people are thinking in terms of the persons they wish to be. Delay of gratification makes sense if it interferes with one's relationship to God or achieving one's purpose. Many tend to believe that the future can be trusted to provide sexual gratification in a marriage relationship. For them, purpose and hope rather than fear of punishment provide the basis for delaying sexual gratification.

Another powerful inhibitor of gratification is the expectation of the community of faith to which the young person belongs. Bettleheim, in *Children of a Dream*, notes the power of unspoken expectations in a Jewish kibbutz. Though housed in coed arrangements and told that sex is natural, children sense very quickly the adult belief that sexual promiscuity interferes with the work and mission of the kibbutz. The expectation of sexual continence, based on community experience with unbridled promiscuity, in early years sharply limits youthful sexual involvement.

A community of faith provides the support group youth need for living in accord with their beliefs; the norms of congregation and home powerfully reinforce a youth's decision to delay sexual gratification until marriage.

American youth and premarital sex. A somewhat different from church youth attitude toward premarital sex emerges for American youth generally. In a 1972 survey of 24,000 student leaders who are juniors and seniors in high school, a total of 71% said they have never engaged in sexual intercourse. On the other hand, among a random group of 393 young people ages 13–19 interviewed the same year, 52% admitted to having had sexual intercourse one or more times (Sorenson 1973).

Age, educational level, and religious faith can account for the difference in percentages between the two studies. Sorenson's study may report a higher incidence of premarital sex because his sample includes 19-year-olds and dropouts from high school. Furthermore, his procedure of asking permission of parents to interview their children on matters of sex may have caused a higher percentage of refusals from church parents. It appears that his small group ($N = 393$) lacks an adequate sampling of church youth, who form the majority of young Americans.

A fair estimate of the numbers involved in premarital sex among American high-school youth, ages 15–18, is a midpoint (40%) between 29% and 52%. It should be understood that in some subcultures, premarital sex is common, whereas in others it is less common. Sorenson, however, sees a trend when he observes that "adolescents are having sexual intercourse at an earlier age than before, and bringing less maturity and less rationality to bed with them." He also takes note of the ease that permits a female sexual adventurer to believe she loves any person she willingly sleeps with; she is apparently able to move in and out of love quite rapidly without confusion or remorse.

Sorenson's interviews showed that mutuality and belonging are emphasized by many young people when describing what love means to them. But they distinguish between a durable love (lifelong and rewarding to family life) and transient love, in which only intense love and a desire for sex are relevant. Such love, whether mono- or multi-affectional, is viewed as existing only for a time, for mutual gratification, with no commitments being made to the other.

The report further indicates that youth view sexual activity as a form of communication, a way of accepting another and in turn feeling accepted. Enhanced relationships, rather than physical experiences, are identified as most important to the youth of Sorenson's sample:

> They look to their sex partners not for what the years ahead hold for each other but for what life has to offer today. Even a single intimate interlude offers comfort and solace to many adolescents; their commitment involves what each can mean to the other at the moment. The values to be realized by such a relationship may not be as enduring or deeply felt as those enjoyed by many married couples, but some self-realization is accomplished in sharing a sexual relationship with another (Sorenson 1973, p. 409).

The relationship between loneliness and premarital sex is seen especially in the youth singled out as sexual adventurers (those who seek many sexual mates). Sorenson found that, of all the sexual behavior groups he studied, sexual adventurers are most in conflict with their parents. Many do not feel they have gotten to know either parent: 58% of all sexual adventurers feel they have never gotten to know their fathers, and 40% believe they have never gotten to know their mothers.

The study concludes that premarital sex is not immoral in the eyes of most young people. For them, sexual activities have no relevance to morality except in the way the activity is used. The objective is intimacy and warmth without any obligation or responsibility. For a large number it is sex without commitment, gratification without obligation, and transient love without promise.

An added comment also seems appropriate.

> We have had premarital and co-marital sex for nearly as long as man can remember with less than spectacular results in deepening the relational values that give significance to human life.
>
> Father Eugene Kennedy

Drug use. In our study we found that loss of faith is more strongly associated with drug abuse, than parent-youth tension or low self-esteem.

This conclusion is based on an analysis of the 14% of the ecumenical sample who, in 1970, admitted to one of the five types of usage listed below. Other surveys in 1970 showed that up to 20% of American youth sometimes used drugs. It is not the percentage of use, but rather the insight into characteristics and needs of users that is important here:

No reference will be made to heroin users because the sample is too small and unrepresentative to warrant generalizations about church youth.

Type of Usage	No. of Youth	Percentage of Sample
Use pot—marijuana—occasionally	511	7
Use pot frequently	162	2
Use pot frequently and have used acid (LSD)	143	2
Have used speed, either alone or with other drugs	115	2
Have used heroin or other hard narcotics	39	1
		14

Following are some of the conclusions that can be drawn from our data and which are supported by other studies.

—Drug users come from less cohesive families than nonusers; they come from homes where parents take a negative stance toward life and themselves. A notable increase in parent-youth conflict occurs when the usage moves from occasional marijuana to speed.

—Drug users are impulsive, with a high tolerance for risk; many have low self-esteem, often disguised as braggadocio.

—Drug users tend to form only superficial friendships, using the ritual of drug use to effect a sense of community. Fewer are identified with God or a congregation, shunning opportunities for growth, service, responsibility, and a life of purpose.

—Drug users are more skeptical about life and mix rebellion and cynicism when relating to home, school, and church. Fewer are positive about their family or congregation.

—Though they agitate for social justice, drug users are more prejudiced and less involved in social action than nonusers.

—Drug users of high-school age are more apt to exhibit low school performance and delinquent behavior. The majority favor premarital sex and getting high on alcohol (e.g., occasional pot users, 70% versus 25% of nonusers).

The close tie between drug usage and loss of faith suggests that religious commitment is, for many, the way of release from drug abuse. Psychotherapy ranks below a religious approach in freeing drug addicts. Teen Challenge, for example, approaches drug addiction as a moral disease and confronts youth with the possibility of release through a religious commitment; their record attests to the ability of religiously committed youth to shoulder moral and ethical responsibility.

Admittedly, factors other than loss of faith are also involved in drug abuse. Addiction is frequently associated with the lack of an effective father figure during childhood; there is a high correlation between indulgent mothers and addiction in their sons. But whatever the causative factors, the therapy that rehabilitates addicts features two ingredients: helping the person to a personal faith and supporting him through a sustaining community. The National Commission on Marijuana and Drug Abuse reported a direct tie between youth's feeling that life has no meaning and their use of drugs. The members of this commission see the growth and development of an ethical system as a necessary solution to the problem of drug abuse.

A striking contrast between church youth and nonchurch youth in regard to drug use comes from a 1970 study of students in a midwestern liberal arts college. Donald Chipman (Providence, Rhode Island, Drug Dependency Treatment Clinic, 1972) and Clyde Parker (University of Minnesota, 1972) began reviewing fifty studies of college drug-use patterns. They found that the national rate for marijuana "ever used" is between 40% and 50%. Since few studies classified students by extent of drug use, Chipman and Parker divided their random sample of 800 students into four groups: (1) regular users of marijuana; (2) casual users; (3) experimental users (e.g., tried it once or twice); and (4) nonusers. They found that the four groups were distinctly different in some areas and quite alike in others.

The most striking contrasts were between group one (regular users) and group four (nonusers). Group one members did not attend church frequently, if at all, and held a wide range of nontraditional as well as agnostic beliefs. Nonusers attended church regularly and espoused traditional beliefs about the supreme deity. Following are other controls:

Frequent Users of Marijuana	*Nonusers of Marijuana*
Highest use of strong and dangerous drugs.	Little use of drugs (except in diet pills).
Highest alcohol usage and for some a problem.	Least use of alcohol.
More active politically.	Least active politically.
Most critical of father's upbringing.	Least critical of father's upbringing.
Lowest grades.	Highest grades.
Most who feel estranged from their families.	Fewest who feel estranged from their families.
Most cynical about life.	Least cynical about life.

The authors identify the nonusers as the most distinctive of the four groups. Members of this group appear well adjusted, show confidence in what they are doing, and are willing to deal with life as they find it. The high correlation between religiosity and nonusage confirms our findings on the probable impact of a personal faith on youth's life-style and world view.

Drinking. Despite the furor over marijuana, LSD, heroin, and tranquilizers, alcohol remains the drug of choice for American teenagers. Authorities on drinking believe that drug abuse has contributed to the fact that deaths from cirrhosis of the liver (a common ailment among heavy drinkers) rose 500% for males, ages 15–24, from 1960 to 1968. Studies of drinking among high-school students in Massachusetts and Mississippi indicate that teenagers with drinking problems make up 2–5% of the adolescent population, or about the same as adults.

Among church youth three out of ten (31%) report sometimes getting high on alcoholic beverages; 15% drink once a week or more often.

The reason for fewer drinkers among church youth is well known (Sebald 1972, p. 42). One's religious culture plays an important role in shaping attitudes and behavior relating to alcoholic beverages. This is seen in the percentage response of youth, when divided by denomination, to items about drinking.

TABLE 15
Drinking by Denomination

Item	Percentage Answering Yes					
	Meth.	Episc.	Cath.	Y.Life	S.Bap.	A.Bap.
	N=522	N=529	N=1818	N=1397	N=917	N=1038
I drink alcoholic beverages						
a. Never	49%	24%	19%	25%	49%	35%
b. Once a year or less	17	15	13	16	15	17
c. Two or three times a yr.	16	23	22	21	13	23
d. About once a month	9	20	22	19	12	16
e. About once a week	5	13	16	11	7	7
f. More than once a week	2	4	8	4	4	1
g. Blank	3	1	1	4	1	2
I sometimes get high on alcoholic beverages	18	34	41	37	22	23

The higher percentage of nonabstainers among Roman Catholic youth (19%) relates to the official lack of injunction against drinking among Catholics. Among Methodist and Southern Baptist youth where most of the clergy oppose or condemn drinking and total abstinence is seen as an expression of moral earnestness, the number of abstainers is nearly half (49%).

Though the use of alcoholic beverages is inversely related to the importance youth accord their faith, there is a significant minority of religiously committed youth who do drink.

	"I sometimes get high on alcohol"
My faith is unimportant	53%
not too important	45
somewhat important	38
quite important	28
very important	22

These are youth who reject regulatory principles and prefer their own experience as the basis for deciding their norms. Their commitment is not to a system, but to a way of being. They are determined to make only those decisions which build confidence in one another and sustain trust between persons. This may or may not result in total abstinence.

For many church youth, however, drinking is associated with less interest in personal faith. Our study indicates that youth who are sometimes high on alcoholic beverages and those who are not show greatest score differences on dimensions relating to religious commitment.

This extended treatment of moral responsibility may look as though the hallmark of Christianity is delay of gratification. It is not. A sense of moral responsibility involves a life of integrity and concern for one's fellowman that bespeaks a life of love. These accents in the life of the committed are highlighted in the two remaining characteristics.

The significance of the previous pages is what they add to the already voluminous literature on youth's involvement in drugs and sex. The new dimension is empirical evidence that a personal faith highly predicts a responsible person who evaluates indulgence in light of his goals and their effects on all concerned.

7. Reaching Out

1. See Roy Fairchild's discussion of Delayed Gratification: A Psychological and religious Analysis, in *Research on Religious Development: A Comprehensive Handbook*, edited by Merton P. Strommen, New York: Hawthorne Press, Inc., 1971, pp. 155–210.

2. This write-up summarizing reports from 91 effective youth leaders was prepared by Dr. Francis Gamelin, President of Higher Education Coordinating Council, St. Louis, Missouri. His account,

found on pp. 7.9–7.12, is found in "Descriptive Studies of Church Youth Workers" published by Youth Research Center.

The 420-item Youth Research Survey, from which much of the data in this book is derived, is available for use by local churches and other youth-serving organizations. It can also be taken by individual young persons, computer-processed, and be interpreted through an individual profile and an accompanying interpretative manual. For information on the Survey and accompanying services, write Youth Research Center, 122 West Franklin Avenue, Minneapolis, Minnesota 55404.

Bibliography

Adorno, T. W.; Frenkel-Brunswik, E.; Levinson, D. J.; and Sanford, R. N. 1950. *The authoritarian personality.* New York: Harper & Row. 2 vols. New York: Wiley, Science Editions, 1964.

Allen, R. O., and Spilka, B. 1967. Committed and consensual religion: a specification of religion-prejudice relationships. *Journal for the scientific study of religion* 6: 191–206.

Allport G. 1954. *The nature of prejudice.* Cambridge, Mass.: Addison-Wesley.

Allport, G., and Ross, J. M. 1967. Personal religious orientation and prejudice. *Journal of personal social psychology* 5: 432–43.

APA Monitor. 1972. Parent/child relationship found in teenage drug use study 3: 8.

Bayer, A. E.; Kent, L.; and Dutton, J. E. 28 June 1972. *Christian century,* pp. 708–13.

Benson, P., and Spilka, B. 1972. God image as a function of self-esteem and locus of control. Paper presented at the International Congress of Learned Societies in the Field of Religion, 5 September 1972, Los Angeles, California.

Bernard, J. 1966. Marital stability and patterns of status variables. *Journal of marriage and family* 28: 423.

Bettelheim, B. 1969. *The children of the dream.* New York: Macmillan.

Burchinal, L. G. 1971. Characteristics of adolescents from unbroken, broken, and reconstituted families. In *Contemporary adolescence: readings,* ed. H. Thornburg. Belmont, Cal.: Brooks/Cole.

Campbell, W. D. 1962. *Race and the renewal of the church.* Philadelphia: Westminster Press.

Chapman, R. 1963. *The loneliness of man.* London: SCM Press Ltd.

Chipman, D. A., II. November 1972. Characteristics of liberal arts college student marijuana users. *Journal of college student personnel,* pp. 511–17.

Corbett, J. M., and Johnson, C. E. 1972. *It's happening with youth.* New York: Harper & Row.

de Lone, R. H. 11 November 1972. The ups and downs of drug-abuse education. *Saturday review of education,* pp. 27–32.

Dentler, R. A. 1967. *Major social problems.* Chicago: Rand McNally.

Dittes, J. E. 1973. *Bias and the pious.* Minneapolis: Augsburg.

Dizmang, L. H. July 1967. Suicide among the Cheyenne Indians. *Bulletin of suicidology,* pp. 8–11.

———. 1970. Indian teen-age suicides shock investigators. *Roche medical image and commentary* 6: 11–13.

Flannery, E. 1965. *Anguish of the Jews: twenty-three centuries of anti-Semitism.* New York: Macmillan.

Forde, G. 1972. *Where God meets man: Luther's down-to-earth approach to the gospel.* Minneapolis: Augsburg.

Goldstein, M. J.; Rodnick, E. H.; Judd, L. L.; and Gould, E. 1970. Galvanic skin reactivity among family groups containing disturbed adolescents. *Journal of abnormal psychology* 1: 57–67.

Gordon, T. 1970. *Parent effectiveness training: the no-lose way to raise children.* New York: Peter H. Wyden.

Grams, A. 1968. *Changes in family life.* St. Louis: Concordia.

Greeley, A. M. 1972. *Unsecular man.* New York: Schocken Books.

Greene, W. 1971. *Youth's agenda for the seventies: a report on the White House Conference on Youth with a summary of the recommendations.* New York: The JDR 3rd Fund.

Habel, N. 1969. *For mature adults only.* Philadelphia: Fortress Press.

Hadden, J. K. 1969. The private generation. *Psychology today* 5: 32.

Hall, G. S. 1904. *Adolescence.* vol. 1. New York: Appleton.

Hanssen, C. A., and Paulson, M. J. 1972. Our anti-establishment youth: revolution or evolution. *Adolescence* 27: 393–408.

Hastings, P. K., and Hage, D. R. 1970. Religious change among college students over two decades. *Social forces* 1: 16–28.

Havighurst, R. J., and Keating, B. 1971. The religion of youth. In *Research on religious development,* ed. M. P. Strommen, pp. 686–723. New York: Hawthorn.

Heath, D. H. 1969. Secularization and maturity of religious beliefs. *Journal of religion and health* 4: 335–58.

Hines, W. 11 July 1972. How 455 in 1,000 marriages break up. *Minneapolis Star.*

Jacobs, J. 1971. *Adolescent suicide.* New York: Wiley.

Johnson, D. W., and Cornell, G. W. 1972. *Punctured preconceptions.* New York: Friendship Press.

Johnston, J., and Bachman, J. 1971. *Young men look at military service: preliminary report.* Ann Arbor: Survey Research Institute, Institute for Social Research, The University of Michigan.

Jorstad, E. 1972. *That new-time religion*. Minneapolis: Augsburg.

Josephson, E., and Josephson, M., eds. 1962. *Man alone: alienation in modern society*. New York: Dell.

Kandel, D. B., and Lesser, G. S. 1972. *Youth in two worlds*. San Francisco: Jossey-Bass.

Kaufman, B. 1972. *Up the down staircase*. New York: Avon.

Keniston, K. 1960. *The uncommitted: alienated youth in American society*. New York: Harcourt.

Klein, D. F. 1972. Youthful rebels—diagnosis and treatment. *Adolescence* 27: 351–69.

Life. 16 May 1969. What people think about their high schools: a survey by Louis Harris.

Little, S. 1968. *Youth, world, and church*. Richmond, Va.: John Knox Press.

McCain, T. Winter 1973. Written before I became a Christian. *Focus on youth* 14: 11.

Marty, M. E. 1958. *The new shape of American religion*. New York: Harper & Bros.

————. 1965. *Youth considers "do-it-yourself" religion*. New York: Thomas Nelson.

Mead, M. 1970. *Culture and commitment: a study of the generation gap*. Garden City, N.Y.: Natural History Press.

Merton, R. K., and Nisbet, R. A., eds. 1961. *Contemporary social problems*. New York: Harcourt, Brace & World.

Minneapolis Star. 22 June 1972. Alcoholism growing as teen-age problem.

Minneapolis Tribune. 6 August 1972. Loneliness, doubt led comedian's son into drug addiction.

Mirthes, C. 1971. *Can't you hear me talking to you?* New York: Bantam Books.

Morris, J. 1965. *Marriage counseling*. Englewood Cliffs, N.J.: Prentice-Hall.

Muuss, R. E. 1962. *Theories of adolescence*. New York: Random House.

National Commission on Marijuana and Drug Abuse. May 1972. Reported in *Youth today* 9: 1.

National Institute of Mental Health. *Clergy-youth counseling project*. Final report. No. MH 16460–01, in press.

Packard, V. 1972. *A nation of strangers*. New York: McKay.

Pedersen, Paul. 1968. Religion as the basis of social change among the Bataks of North Sumatra. Ph.D. dissertation, Claremont Graduate School.

Randers, J., and Meadows, D. H. 1972. The carrying capacity of the globe. *Sloan management review* 2: 11–27.

Reich, C. A. 1970. *The greening of America.* New York: Random House.

Rogers, J. M. 1971. Drug abuse, just what the doctor ordered. *Psychology today* 5: 24.

Rokeach, M. 1960. *The open and closed mind.* New York: Basic Books.

Rosenberg, M. 1965. *Society and the adolescent self-image.* Princeton: Princeton Univ. Press.

Sabine, G. 1971. *When you listen, this is what you can hear.* Iowa City, Iowa: ACT Publications.

Schechter, M. D., and Sternlof, R. E. 1970. Suicide in adolescents. *Postgraduate medicine* 5: 220–23.

Sebald, H. 1968. *Adolescence: a sociological analysis.* New York: Appleton-Century-Crofts.

————. 1972. The pursuit of "instantness" in technocratic society and youth's psychedelic drug use. *Adolescence* 27: 343–50.

Seiden, R. H. 1966. Campus tragedy: a study of student suicide. *Journal of abnormal psychology* 6: 389–99.

————. 1969. Suicide among youth. A report prepared for the Joint Commission on Mental Health of Children. A supplement to the *Bulletin of suicidology.* Washington, D.C.: U.S. Government Printing Office.

Shannon, Bishop J. P. 12 November 1972. The pilgrim church. *Minneapolis Tribune.*

Sorenson, R. C. 1973. *Adolescent sexuality in contemporary America.* New York: World.

Strommen, M. P. 1963. *Profiles of church youth.* St. Louis: Concordia.

————. 1973. *Bridging the gap.* Minneapolis: Augsburg.

Strommen, M. P., ed. 1971. *Research on religious development: a comprehensive handbook.* New York: Hawthorn.

Strommen, M. P., and Gupta, R. K. 1971. *Manual for youth research survey: section 4.* Minneapolis: Youth Research Center.

Strommen, M. P.; Brekke, M. L.; Underwager, R. C.; and Johnson, A. L. 1972. *A study of generations.* Minneapolis: Augsburg.

The United Presbyterian Church in the U.S.A. 1970. *The world of church youth: a study of United Presbyterian youth and their leaders, parents and pastors.* Philadelphia: Board of Christian Education, The United Presbyterian Church in the U.S.A.

Time. 21 August 1972. Teen-age sex: letting the pendulum swing, p. 34.

U.S. News & World Report. 9 August 1971. End of the "youth revolt"? Survey of changing mood, pp. 26–31.

Weddige, R. L., and Steinhilber, R. M. 1971. Attempted suicide by drug overdose. *Postgraduate medicine: the journal of applied medicine* 5: 184–86.

Who's Who among American High School Students. December 1972. Results of annual survey reported in *Youth today*.

Woodyard, D. O. 1969. *To be human now*. Philadelphia: Westminster Press.

Wrenn, C. G. 1973. *The world of the contemporary counselor*. Boston: Houghton Mifflin.

Yankelovich, D. 1969. What they believe: a *Fortune* survey. In *Youth in turmoil*. New York: Time-Life.